HEALING
HEARTS

HEALING HEARTS

A leading pediatric heart surgeon learns about

THE JOURNEY FROM GRIEF TO LIFE

from these inspiring mothers of his lost patients

HISASHI NIKAIDOH, MD

with JANIS LEIBS DWORKIS

AMBASSADOR INTERNATIONAL
GREENVILLE, SOUTH CAROLINA & BELFAST, NORTHERN IRELAND

www.ambassador-international.com

Healing Hearts

ISBN: 978-1-62020-128-2 (paperback)
eISBN: 978-1-62020-180-0 (digital)

Cover design and typesetting: Matthew Mulder
E-book conversion: Anna Riebe

AMBASSADOR INTERNATIONAL
Emerald House
427 Wade Hampton Blvd.
Greenville, SC 29609, USA
www.ambassador-international.com

AMBASSADOR BOOKS
The Mount
2 Woodstock Link
Belfast, BT6 8DD, Northern Ireland, UK
www.ambassadormedia.co.uk

The colophon is a trademark of Ambassador

Praise be to the God and Father of our Lord Jesus Christ, the Father of compassion and the God of all comfort, who comforts us in all our troubles, so that we can comfort those in any trouble with the comfort we ourselves have received from God.

2 Corinthians 1:3-4

New International Version

TABLE OF CONTENTS

FOREWORD

BY

C. EVERETT KOOP, MD, ScD

FORMER SURGEON GENERAL OF THE UNITED STATES

I PROBABLY SHOULD BE FLATTERED by the number of folks who ask me to write a preface, a forward, or a blurb for the jacket of the book they are writing. As a matter of fact, I've come to the time of my life when I have to say a reluctant "no," unless I have been involved in the subject myself.

The whole question has a very practical side because the keenest surgeon, the most accomplished internist, is not always intellectually, psychologically, and emotionally equipped to steer the family of a dying child over the rocky road, let alone the many barriers that occur in a family after the death of a child.

No one really "enjoys" the doctor's role in the doctor/patient relationship surrounding death, near death, and death's aftermath. I became interested particularly in the role of the physician in "peri-thanatology" after the second Christmas I was in the practice of pediatric surgery. My wife and I were going over the Christmas cards I received from patients' parents and to my amazement, the largest cohort of six sympathetic letters came from parents of children who had died the previous year.

I remember talking with Dr. Nikaidoh and saying that I would probably like best the stories told by mothers who had lost their children but who had recovered to lead a life of human service to others—especially if told in their own simple expressions (rather than more sophisticated rhetoric). When our family lost its youngest member at twenty in what the world called a mountain-climbing accident, Betty, his mother, and I wrote the book *Sometimes Mountains Move*, which was nothing more than the story of the working of a Christian God in our lives at the time of our deepest distress. Folks representing many religions who read this book after losing a child lamented the randomness of their own child's association with an untimely death.

After talking with Dr. Nikaidoh, I felt that his book would send a clear message about "a plan beyond human understanding," i.e. "the Sovereignty of God."

Books of this genre, and especially this book of Dr. Nikaidoh's, are a testimony to the power of God without the appearance of preaching. Dr. Nikaidoh is not ashamed of this gospel for "it is God's power for salvation to everyone who believes . . ." (Romans 1:16).

C. Everett Koop, MD, ScD
U.S. Surgeon General 1981-1989
Hanover, NH

"It was ten weeks after David died when his Bible came into our hands. We had been told by his brothers that his bookmark was in Jude, and presumably, this was the last Scripture passage he had read. David's Bible is Revised Standard Version, and in that particular edition, the book of Jude ends on the left hand page with only one full verse, the last one. We opened his Bible and read the last thing that he had read: 'And now unto him who is able to keep you from falling....' God was able, but in His sovereignty He chose not to."

C. Everett and Elizabeth Koop
Sometimes Mountains Move
Tyndale House Publishers, Inc,
1979

Dr. C. Everett Koop

1916-2013

ACKNOWLEDGEMENTS

THIS BOOK COULD NOT have been written without the kindness, honesty, and spiritual generosity of the mothers who were willing to bare their souls for this project. All of us wish to avoid the enormous grief they have experienced, and our hearts go out to them. I know their willingness to share such raw emotions will benefit so many others—who will now know they are not alone as they, too, walk this path of grief. I am also grateful to these mothers for sharing the details of their "recovery" and the healing they received from helping others.

I would like to thank Ms. Janis Leibs Dworkis, a professional writer and close friend of my beloved wife, Lynn. Janis worked tirelessly on multiple versions of this manuscript while keeping in close communication with each contributing mother and with me. The subject matter of this book is personal to Janis, too, as she lost her brother to leukemia in his adult life.

We began collecting the mothers' stories in the summer of 2007, and our initial interviews were concluded in the spring of 2008. The long and arduous search for a publisher ended in February 2012, when Mr. Sam Lowry of Ambassador International gave us the opportunity to send this book out into the world. I am grateful for his kind and gentle treatment of this unknown author. I want to thank Mr. Tim Lowry, whose attention to the details of publishing and the book's timeline has been deeply appreciated. I am also grateful for the superb editorial work of Ms. Brenda Covert and truly artistic design of the cover and interior by Mr. Matthew Mulder.

There are so many doctors, nurses, respiratory therapists, other medical professionals, chaplains /people of the clergy, and social workers who contributed to the care of the children whose lives are described in this book. I am deeply grateful to them all. For the sake of fairness and privacy, I intentionally omitted all individual names and meant no disrespect to anyone. The vast majority of events described in this book occurred at Children's Medical Center of Dallas where I was privileged to work for 31 years. I am very grateful to the administrative staff and the board who have built and maintained such a superb hospital for children.

Finally, but not least, I am deeply indebted to my wife of 34 years. Lynn has been my true friend, strong advocate, and unflinching supporter. In the long, stretched-out process of making this book, her encouragement has been constant and far beyond my words of gratitude.

I am thankful to our Sovereign God whose love and mercy we cannot live without.

Hisashi Nikaidoh, MD

CHAPTER 1

HISASHI NIKAIDOH

I WAS ELEVEN YEARS OLD when I decided to become a doctor. I remember the day. I remember the moment. But most of all, I remember the wonderful feeling I had—the deeply satisfying feeling of being of service to another human being.

I have lived more than sixty years since that day, every one of them spent in the pursuit or practice of medicine. How I wish I could say that I kept that ideal of service in the forefront of my vision during each of those years. But the truth is quite different. Life is a journey, after all, and sometimes it takes extraordinary events and challenges to bring us back to our original vision.

I grew up as the son of a physician. I took it for granted at the time, just as most children take their parents' professions for granted. But I realize now that when my father announced his career decision to his own parents, he must have seemed nothing short of a rebel. After all, stretching directly behind my father were twelve consecutive generations of Buddhist priests. And before them, twelve generations of samurai warriors. But in the face of this extensive and distinguished family history, my father felt called to serve on a different path. He followed his heart, and I doubt he ever looked back.

My father's medical clinic was located in Tokyo, where he,

my mother, my siblings, and I lived during my earliest childhood. But in 1943, when I was eight years old, the Allied bombing of Japan increased, and all "non-essential" citizens were told to evacuate the city. My mother and father both stayed in Tokyo. But in the spring of that year, my siblings and I were sent away to the countryside.

We went to live with an aunt on the land that had been granted to one of our samurai ancestors in the thirteenth century, near Sukagawa in northern Japan. The plan was that we would stay in our ancestral home—a thatched-roof house on a farm with an open fire pit and an outdoor well—until it was safe to move back to Tokyo. As it turned out, however, we lived there for seven years, well beyond the end of World War II.

From the moment I arrived at the farm, my life as I had known it ended definitively, and a completely new life began. My new days began before dawn as I watered the rice paddies for an hour or more. After school, it was my job to heat the bathhouse water. First, I made sixteen trips with two buckets from the well to the bathhouse. Then, once the bath was full, I tended the fire for hours to heat the water. I also fed the rabbits, chickens, and sheep. In the fall, I collected the leaves to make compost. In the spring, I tilled and planted the vegetable garden.

It was hard work for such a young child, and I missed my parents terribly. But I knew better than to cry or complain. In the Japanese culture of that time, it was absolutely unacceptable for boys of any age to express feelings of pain or sadness, no matter what we were experiencing. Had my brothers or I displayed such emotion, we would have been considered unworthy to be boys. So we did our jobs, we kept our sadness inside, and we waited to go home.

Instead, as it turned out, "home" came to us. In April 1945, just a few months before the war ended, my father's Tokyo clinic was destroyed in a bombing raid. Forty-three years old at the time, he was immediately drafted to become an army surgeon and was told he would be shipped to Manchuria. But while he waited to be shipped out, the war ended. With his Tokyo clinic in ruins, he and my mother came out to our ancestral home to live with us.

We children were thrilled that our family was safe and together again. But we were also aware that my father had lost his clinic and his livelihood. Without medical instruments or medications, he had no means to practice his profession in the countryside. Only as an adult was I able to look back and understand the devastation he must have felt.

Nevertheless, although my father was not officially practicing medicine, I noticed that people still came to him when they were ill. And he graciously did what he could to be helpful. Sometimes, people would come to our house for help. Sometimes he treated sick people in their homes, and occasionally he gave public health talks—all for a very small fee, if anything.

One day when I was eleven years old, my father asked for my help. Among his patients at that time was a little boy with a bone infection in his leg. Under normal circumstances, my father would have treated the infection with antibiotics and given the child something for pain. But without medication of any kind, the best he could do was to try to keep the wound clean. My job was to hold a pan under the boy's leg and make sure he didn't move suddenly as my father washed the area, occasionally picking out a piece of dead bone from the depth of the wound.

The little boy, not more than six years old, must have been in quite a bit of pain. I, too, was uncomfortable and even a bit squeamish at first. But I was honored that my father had chosen me to be his helper, and I tried very hard to keep everything as still as possible, just as he asked.

I watched my father carefully as he worked under such primitive conditions, trying to be gentle while thorough. I sensed both his sincere concern for the boy's wellbeing and his own satisfaction that he could be of help in some way.

As for me, I experienced a brand new feeling that day—my own sense of pleasure from being of service to another human being. I liked that feeling. At age eleven, I decided I wanted that to be a permanent part of my life.

From that moment on, my life was focused on becoming a doctor and driven by the statistics of my chances.

First, I would be required to take an exam to enter a college as a pre-med student, an exam that would eliminate more than 95 percent of the applicants. Once making it into the pre-med pool, I would later take another exam that would weed out more than 80 percent of those remaining. That meant that of all the high school students like me who wanted to study medicine, only one out of every one hundred would make it into medical school.

Competition became the framework of my world. I didn't care how hard I had to work or what I had to sacrifice. In every single class, in every single assignment, I would not accept less than perfection from myself. I was determined to become that one student out of one hundred.

In 1954, I entered medical school at Tokyo University, the most prestigious university in Japan at that time. Once again, competition was everything to me. During all my classes, all my rotations, I would accept nothing less than perfection from myself. I graduated in 1959 and did my rotating internship at the U.S. Naval Hospital in Yokosuka, Japan.

Now I was a doctor. I had attained my goal. But what did I find after so many years of fierce competition, pressure, and a constant fear of failure? I found disappointment. Yes, I was a physician, but I found no satisfaction in it. I kept asking myself, What was I actually *doing?* I had discovered that our bodies are blessed with a powerful healing mechanism. And while I was certainly grateful for that, I didn't want to simply administer medicine and then stand by and watch the body heal itself. *I* wanted to be the healer. Wasn't that what I had worked so hard for? I wanted the healing to be a direct result of *my* action, *my* personal intervention.

I decided to go into surgery.

At that time, American medicine was considered the best in the world—and I wanted the best. Although our countries had been at war only fifteen years earlier, and although that war had caused my own family many hardships, when I told my father of my desire to study in the U.S., he was not against the plan. He was a well-educated man who understood the world and the stature of the United States in that world. So in 1960, I left Japan to begin my five-year residency in general surgery at Mount Sinai Hospital in New York City.

Not surprisingly, I once again worked hard, sacrificed much, and accepted nothing less than perfection from myself. I found tremendous satisfaction in learning and applying surgical techniques, in playing a hands-on role in the healing of my patients.

But at the end of that five-year residency, what did I find?

I found disappointment. Yes, I certainly enjoyed surgery more than medicine. I enjoyed the practice of taking action, of making things happen. But once again, I asked myself, What was I actually *doing?* If I operated on a man who was seventy-five years old, how much of a difference did I really make? How much longer was he realistically going to live—with or without my intervention? Or suppose I removed the gallbladder of a middle-aged woman. How much of a difference was that surgery really making in the world? Whatever it was, it didn't feel like enough to me. I wanted to make the most significant impact possible.

I looked to pediatric surgery. If I could operate on a child, wouldn't I be making a difference that would last a *long* lifetime, a difference that would be valued by the child and the parents for years to come?

So on top of my one-year internship and five-year general surgery residency, I decided to add a two-year residency in pediatric surgery at Children's Memorial Hospital in Chicago. Again, I worked to be the best, to accept nothing less than perfection from myself.

But after that residency and after having practiced general pediatric surgery for several years, where was I once again? I was back at disappointment. I was never satisfied. It was never enough. I was driven by the need for a greater challenge and a way for *me* to make a greater impact.

This time, I looked to pediatric heart surgery. Maybe that would quell my desire for power, my need to be *the* healer. So at the age of forty, I went back and did a one-year additional residency in thoracic surgery at Case Western Reserve University.

By 1975, at the end of that residency, I had obtained three specialty board certifications: general surgery, pediatric surgery, and cardiothoracic surgery. While it might look impressive on paper, no doctor actually needs three board certifications! I was exceedingly over-qualified for almost everything. What was I doing? What had I done?

One thing is certain: I had all but forgotten the wonderful feeling of service that had stirred my young soul that day on the farm. In all those intervening years of intense study and practice and constant striving for perfection, I had overlooked my initial reason for becoming a physician—in my opinion the only *true* reason—compassion for the suffering of others. Although I looked impressive on paper, my professional life was actually a mess.

Perhaps not surprisingly, my personal life suffered as well.

In 1962, while I was in my general surgery residency at Mount Sinai Hospital, I married Peggy Stewart in New York. From the beginning, there were difficulties to overcome. My in-laws refused to bless their daughter's marriage to a Japanese man, and they did not show up at our wedding. Even as my mother-in-law neared the end of her battle with cancer the following year, and I went to visit her in the hospital, or when I attended her wake and funeral, my presence brought only discomfort and pain to my new extended family.

Our first son, Makoto, was born in Chicago in 1966, just after I finished my general surgery residency. After his birth, the three of us moved to Japan, and I returned to my alma mater, Tokyo University Medical School, where I taught. In 1968, our second son, Hitoshi, was born.

Soon after my return to Japan, the medical students went on strike to reform the old regime of the university. Several hundred students barricaded themselves in the clock tower at the campus.

I listened to the students' concerns and found that I agreed with them. Unfortunately, the chancellor made a different decision. He chose to call in riot police to physically rout out the students instead of listening to their point of view. That action made me feel so isolated, disappointed, and disillusioned that I decided I really couldn't work in such an environment. I resigned my position. Peggy, the boys, and I moved back to Chicago, and I began my practice in pediatric surgery at Children's Memorial Hospital. Our third son, Takashi, was born later that year.

It was about five years later when I decided to do my residency in cardiothoracic surgery at Case Western Reserve in Cleveland. I knew it would be only a one-year commitment, and I wanted the five of us to move to Cleveland for the year. But my wife argued that she and the boys should stay in Evanston, the Chicago suburb where we lived. After all, it was a wonderful neighborhood, and the boys' elementary school was less than a block away. In the end, I agreed. I would have preferred to have my family with me. But driven as I was, I would not give up the opportunity for this third residency. I went ahead to Cleveland by myself.

I arranged my schedule so that I could be home from Friday night to Sunday night every third weekend. It was the best I could do. I enjoyed my boys so much and hated being separated from them. At least we had those weekends together. But after several months, Peggy complained that my visits were too painful, too disruptive to her schedule with the boys, and she asked me not to come home so often. At the time, I thought I was doing the right thing by respecting her wishes. So I began to come home less frequently.

My family was not expecting me on Christmas weekend of that year, but I decided to surprise them. I made my way to Evanston through a blinding snowstorm and arrived home at two o'clock in the morning. I arrived to find a man in my home with my wife.

I can't even describe my shock at finding out that my wife had been having an affair with this man for months—in my home *with my children in the house.* I was absolutely sickened and disgusted by her behavior. Apparently, when I originally left for Cleveland, Peggy had told the boys that I had abandoned them and that I was not coming back. She absolutely knew that was not true. But the children were young, and they didn't know what to believe. They felt that I had abandoned them. They were devastated, as was I.

At the end of June 1975, when my residency in Cleveland ended, I moved out of my home into an apartment near Children's Memorial Hospital in Chicago. My boys were five, seven, and nine years old when my divorce from their mother was finalized.

My separation from my wife was humiliating to me, and I was hesitant to tell anyone. In fact, during the time of that separation, I met a scrub nurse named Lynn Graham who worked in the cardiac operating room. Lynn and I were friendly, but I kept my separation a secret because I was so ashamed. We worked together for the next two and a half years and occasionally ran into each other outside of the hospital. We were friendly, but had no romantic relationship.

Then in January 1978, I left Chicago to accept a position at Children's Medical Center in Dallas, Texas. A few weeks later, I went back to Chicago to finish up some personal business and ran into Lynn in the hospital foyer. Later that year, she called to thank me for a recommendation that I had given her and told me it had led to a promotion. By that time, she knew about my divorce, and she shared with me that she was in the process of her own divorce. A few months later, I invited Lynn to Dallas for a weekend—and that's when our romantic relationship began. Within the year, we were married. Within the next five years, we were blessed with the birth of our daughter Kimi and then our son Ken.

So there I was.

I was now in a wonderful marriage to a remarkable woman and was the father of five healthy children. I was a successful surgeon with three board certifications. I performed life-saving surgeries on tiny hearts the size of walnuts. I made an enormous difference in the lives of those patients and in the lives of their parents. I should have been tremendously satisfied with my life.

But there was only one problem: Patients died.

Like any surgeon, like any doctor, I could not save everyone, no matter what I did. But each time one of my patients died, I took it as a sign of devastating personal failure. Children were dying because of my shortcomings. Children were dying because I was not perfect. Children were dying because of *me*.

So, I responded to this problem the same way I had responded to all challenges in my life up to this point. I dedicated myself to perfection. I told myself that if I could just learn enough, practice enough, work hard enough every minute, I would approach perfection in treating my patients. I would have good results all the time. No one would die.

But of course, that was simply not possible.

In those days, the 1970s, we had relatively high mortality rates in pediatric heart surgery compared to today. I did an average of about one surgery every workday and I lost about one patient every two weeks. After each loss, I would become despondent and demoralized for the next two weeks. It doesn't take a lot of math to realize that at those rates, I would have been depressed and miserable all the time. And that's exactly what showed up in my life.

I was always irritable, always exacting. I was so harsh with other people, constantly demanding better performance from my co-workers. I needed them to be perfect. Those who couldn't complain back to me—nurses and residents—received my harshest criticism. I find it difficult to look back at my behavior during that time. It was absolutely shameful.

Then in the early 1980s, two significant events in my life caused me to change my view—and my behavior.

First, I became a Christian.

Growing up, my mother was a Christian, but my father was a Buddhist and would not allow Christianity in our home. I learned about Christianity in college, as I studied all kinds of religions and philosophies, but I never took it personally to heart. When I married Lynn, I wasn't practicing any religion. We joined a Lutheran Church because she was a Christian and it was important to her. When our children were born, she would take them to church. Eventually, I started going with her and then taking some classes. But I was a stubborn man, and it was a long process.

Then, in April 1983, I had a personal conversion experience. Many people say that when they become a Christian, everything in life changes drastically. But not for me. For me, change occurred very, very slowly.

My second life-changing event began with the death of two young patients within a ten-day period a few months after my religious conversion. Neither of these children had a heart problem that should have led to mortality. I was absolutely devastated by these losses. For the first three or four days after the second child died, I could not work at all. I would drive to the hospital and walk in, but before I could get to my office, I would break down sobbing in a hallway. It was all I could do to turn around and go home.

I was terrified. I was absolutely panicked that I would never be able to work again. Then I became so depressed that I thought of quitting cardiac surgery all together. I started thinking about the fact that I was still board certified in pediatric surgery. Maybe that's what I should practice, general pediatric surgery. Maybe I should never touch a child's heart again.

About a week after the second death, my panic reached a crescendo. I felt immobilized and incapacitated. I knew that Lynn was worried about me as well. So I called my pastor to say that I needed to see him right away. But to my surprise, he said he was too busy to see me right then. I was shocked that my pastor was not available in my desperate time of need, but I called a friend of mine who was a chaplain at another hospital. He told me to come right over, and I did. When I got to his office, I absolutely poured my heart out to this man. I cried and I talked. And I cried some more. I was beside myself with misery and pain. My friend listened attentively. I had no idea how much time had gone by, but I finally felt spent.

When I stopped talking, he said, "What Bible verse can you think of right now?"

That certainly was not what I had expected him to say at that moment. Nevertheless, I answered with the only verse that came to mind. "Be still and know that I am God" (Psalm 46:10).

Then the chaplain stood up and held out his hand to shake my own. "Good," he said. "Meditate on that, Dr. Nikaidoh. I'm glad you came in."

This man was dismissing me, and I was incredulous. I came to his office in tears and cried my heart out. I poured my deepest fears out to him. And he asks me one simple question and sends me out! What kind of counseling is that? How could he do that to me?

But he had been very clear that our meeting was over. I was confused and heartsick. But I left and went home.

The following Monday, I decided to try again to go to the hospital. This time, I walked in through a different entrance so I would not have to face too many people. I made it into my office without breaking down. And on my desk, I found two letters sitting side by side. One was written by the minister who had been with me as I counseled the parents of one of the deceased children. The other was written by a nurse who had observed how distraught I was. Both of these individuals recognized the pain I had been in and took the time to write to me, strongly encouraging me to stay with my practice.

And *that* was the moment when I realized that I was not in this alone. God's hand had always been part of the healing process—just as He had brought those two letters to me exactly when I needed them so badly.

At that moment, I finally knew that I did not carry the weight of those children's lives on my shoulders alone. "Be still and know that I am God." In my epiphany, I realized that I did *not* have to be perfect in order to save them. My medical decisions and my surgical practice had never been the only factors in determining life or death for them. God's hand had always been a part of the process. But since I had lacked any sense of humility at all—since I had assumed everything was *about me*—I had been too blind to see it. At that exact moment, I finally felt the relief I had needed so badly. I finally found the peace that my striving for perfection could never bring.

Several months later, I was speaking to our hospital's director of social work when she mentioned she had noticed a change in me. Immediately worrying that it was a change for the worse, I asked her what she meant.

"You used to blame yourself so much whenever anything bad happened," she said. "You don't do that quite so much anymore. That's nice."

And from that time on, I began to build an awareness of that change within myself. I no longer looked at life and death as being all about *me*—what *I* did, what *I* should have done, what *I* should not have done, etc. My newfound faith and understanding of God's hand in our lives had brought me to a place of greater freedom. Now that I was no longer feeling the burden and judgment of perfection, I felt a greater sense of freedom to be the best physician and surgeon I could possibly be and to more fully enjoy my work. I would always do the absolute best that I could for my patients and for their families—but I finally realized that my role as a physician could only go so far. The rest was truly up to God.

About ten years later, another experience helped me further refine and understand my role as a physician.

When my son Ken was in confirmation class at our church, he and his classmates went once a month to the Denton State School about twenty-five miles north of Dallas. I went along as well. This is a residential facility for about 650 people, most of whom have severe and profound mental retardation and many of whom are also medically fragile. The members of Ken's confirmation class would help bring the residents to the school's chapel for Sunday services. After Ken finished confirmation, I decided to continue to volunteer there. So for almost ten years, the school's pastor, myself, and a few of the highest functioning residents helped push those in wheelchairs to Sunday service.

Through those years, a wonderful thing happened. The more time I spent at the Denton State School, the more I realized that the residents there were not really so different from the rest of us. In fact, someone pointed out to me that the only real difference is that most of us can hide our infirmities—but these people cannot.

That immediately made such good sense to me. I had originally thought I was there to serve them. I thought I was doing them a favor, bringing them to the chapel. Instead, they ended up doing a far greater favor for me: They let me know that I am broken too. If I truly acknowledge that I am broken, then I cannot be the mighty and powerful doctor speaking down to the patient in the bed. I cannot be the perfect one bringing healing to those who are imperfect and powerless. No. The truth is that we are all imperfect. We are all broken.

Unfortunately, medicine today is often practiced as if the "rich" doctor is giving part of his wealth as a benevolence to the "poor" patient. But how can that relationship promote healing when there is so much human arrogance in the way? If you imagine that you're the big person reaching down to help the little person—as opposed to sharing in the pain of brokenness we all face in some form—then the effort you make to help is emotionally shallow and eventually self-promoting.

During the years that I volunteered at the Denton State School, my son Hitoshi had graduated from college and was applying to medical school. Of my five children, Hitoshi had decided at a very young age that he wanted to become a physician. Unfortunately, however, his college years were an emotionally difficult time for him, and he did not end up with the grades he needed to get into medical school. Instead, he took a job in a hospital as a blood-drawing technician and then became a technician in the cardiac catheterization lab, a position that provided on-the-job training. Not only did he enjoy working in that lab, but he also showed remarkable progress in knowledge, skills, and even teaching ability. With his skills, reliability, and kind-ness to patients and their family members, he quickly became a "star" technician. But he never gave up his dream to become a physician. So while he was working full time, he attended classes at nearby colleges and universities to bring up his grade-point average.

Hitoshi was thirty-one years old when he was finally ac-cepted to medical school. I was so impressed with his tenacity and so proud of his accomplishments that I made a deal with him: I would pay his tuition and living expenses during medi-cal school, and he would pay me back after graduation. Hitoshi entered the University of Texas Medical School at Houston in 1999.

Not too long after school started, Hitoshi was in an acci-dent while riding his bicycle and was found unconscious by the roadside. Thankfully, he regained consciousness and made a full recovery. While he was in the hospital, several of his classmates brought him daily materials from lectures so he would not be left behind. Toshi noticed that these students seemed consis-tently calm, in spite of threatening exams and tests that clearly rattled most medical students. When he asked them why they were so relaxed, they answered by inviting him to the Baptist Student Union to show him the source of their peace. What he discovered there resulted in his transformation from a formally practicing Catholic into a new creation—a born-again, Christ-seeking disciple of the Teacher. When Lynn and my daughter Kimi visited Houston not too long afterward, Hitoshi told them that he had invited Jesus into his heart for the first time.

Hitoshi was transformed. He organized a weekly men's Bible study, and more than half of his male classmates attended—completely unheard of in medical school! He volunteered in his Catholic Church as a youth leader. He even took a few dozen junior high school students to Colorado for a ski trips. During spring break of his second year in medical school, he went to Venezuela with about two dozen classmates to vaccinate chil-dren in remote villages. He worked with all Houston hospitals to make sure they donated materials to MediSend, an organization that sends the supplies to hospitals and clinics in developing countries. As the president of the Student InterCouncil (representing students throughout all six schools of the campus), he was instrumental in establishing the first free medical clinic for the homeless—and he served there every Sunday. In addition to all this service work, Hitoshi was an active runner, cyclist, and swimmer, running marathons at least once a year and competing in triathlons as well. And somehow, he consistently managed to come to Dallas for every important family event.

On top of it all, Hitoshi was a star student. He was the first student to be called any time the teaching faculty needed help. He was the resource student for medical students who were junior to him.

Toward the end of his years in medical school, Hitoshi made the decision to become a surgeon. Naturally, many people assumed that I influenced that decision. But I absolutely did not. His decision was influenced by Don Meier, MD, chief of surgery at Children's Medical Center of Dallas when Hitoshi did his clinical rotation there. Dr. Meier had served as a missionary surgeon in Nigeria for more than ten years before returning to Dallas to accept a surgical faculty position. After getting to know Hitoshi and his commitment to service, it was Dr. Meier who encouraged him to pursue a surgical career—with the understanding that Hitoshi could split his time equally between general surgery and his missionary work. Hitoshi knew this type of arrangement would result in 50 percent less income than that of an ordinary surgeon, but that never bothered him. He had found his calling, and he never looked back.

When Hitoshi earned his MD degree in 2003, his classmates awarded him their highest honor, the "Gold-Headed Cane Award for Humanism in Medicine." The cane was inscribed as follows: "Humility, Humanity, and Fidelity to Honor the Art of Medicine." Our entire family could not have been more proud of Hitoshi's determination to enter medical school, his persistence during repeated rejection, his hard work and dedication, and most importantly, his humanity. We knew he would go on to do great things for people. I felt strongly that Hitoshi, unlike me, would *not* forget the true nature of a physician's calling to serve.

After graduation, Toshi began his residency at Christus St. Joseph Hospital in Houston—the next step in his journey to become a surgeon. A few weeks later, on a Saturday morning in August, he stepped into one of the hospital elevators. Earlier that week, this particular car had been under repair. Until that moment, no one knew that the repair had not been properly completed. Just as my son stepped into the elevator, the car malfunctioned. Dr. Hitoshi Nikaidoh was killed instantly.

I do not know how I lived through those first few weeks.

Memorial services were held for Hitoshi all over the country—at his church in Houston, at the hospital in Houston where he had just started his residency, at his church in Dallas, at several hospitals in Dallas, at his college in Pennsylvania, and at the boarding school in Connecticut he attended before college. At each place we went, at each service we attended, we were amazed by the remarkable impressions Hitoshi had left in people's hearts.

Hitoshi left behind parents, siblings, nieces, a nephew, cousins, patients, co-workers, classmates, church friends, pastors, roommates—so many people who were touched by the goodness of his life as well as the pain of his death. Our faith teaches us that we will see our son again in heaven, for which I am immeasurably grateful. But as God created us, He also knows that such a loss is filled with pain and suffering for us right here on earth.

Not knowing what else to do to soothe my grief, I went back to work about two weeks after my son's death. My colleagues worried about me and wanted me to take more time off. But I felt that I could not. Taking care of my patients was a full-time job. I hoped that the work would force me to walk away from my grieving. I hoped that the passing time would ease my pain as I continued to work. But being back at work brought its own problems, the most difficult of which was seeing young surgical residents in the doctor's lounge or in the hallways. Any of these images could have been Hitoshi, and a sudden wave of sadness and tears would hit me.

Before Hitoshi died, I always kept a respectful distance between myself and the grieving parents whose children had been my patients. I never said to them, "I understand how painful this must be for you." I knew that I did not understand their pain. Instead, I would say, "I wouldn't dare to assume that I have any idea how painful this is for you. All I can say is that I know it must be terribly painful. And I am so sorry."

But after my own son died, I started looking at things differently. I began to understand certain things that I never could have known. For example, I realized that these parents were not only mourning the child they had loved and lost, the child they had known. They were also mourning the child as they imagined him or her to be in the future. They were mourning all the lost opportunities that would never come to be, the lost potential that would never be fulfilled. Their hopes and dreams for their child, and the hopes and dreams they shared together.

I thought of all the dreams so many of us had had for Hitoshi on his graduation from medical school—those few short weeks before his death. He and I had dreamed about working together on mission trips years from now, with him as the primary surgeon and me as his assistant. That was a future so close to my heart.

While I was better able to understand the many grieving parents I worked with, and while I did what I could to reflect that understanding in my relationships with them, I soon began to wonder what *they* knew that I had not yet learned. I began to feel a burning need inside myself to discover what *they* might know that could help *me*. What could they teach me that would ease my pain?

As that question stayed with me day and night, I began to think back to an experience I had had years earlier. I had been standing outside the hospital cafeteria when I saw a familiar face

and immediately recognized Linda Ojeda, a woman who had
lost her son at this hospital years before from a tragic accident.
Although I had not been involved in his case professionally, I
had seen Linda at her son's bedside every day as I checked on my
own patients in the ICU. It was odd to see her at the hospital
again after so many years. We smiled and acknowledged each
other, then went our separate ways. I realized she must be at the
hospital visiting someone.

A few weeks later, I saw her in the hallway again. And then
again. And again. Each time, we would smile and nod. Finally,
one day, Linda stopped for a moment to talk. With her genuine smile and her open manner, she simply said to me, "Dr.
Nikaidoh, I work here now."

"Oh, wow," I said. "That's very nice."

Those were the only words I could say right then, but so
many chaotic thoughts ran around in my mind. Why would a
mother come to work at the institution that had not been able
to save her son's life? Why would she choose to come to work
every single day in the place where her baby died? Why would
she put herself through that?

As I struggled with my own grief, I kept thinking about that
encounter and another incident the year after I saw Linda. I was
working in the ICU when a new nurse walked in. I looked up
and was shocked to discover that the nurse was Julie Lackey. Her
daughter Kimberly had been a patient of mine in the 1980s. Not
only had I not been able to save her daughter's life, but Julie had
suffered an additional, completely unforeseen tragedy just months
after Kimberly's death. Now Julie worked in the same ICU where
she had lost her precious daughter. How was that possible?

At the time that I had seen Linda and then Julie, I was deeply
intrigued by the fact that they chose to work in a place that I
imagined to be so suffused with pain for them. But I didn't even
think of asking them directly the many questions that were on
my mind. I didn't have the nerve to approach such a delicate
topic. But I do remember thinking that if *I* had lost a child, I
was sure I would want to go far, far away from the location of

such a tragic loss.

Those encounters with Linda and Julie were constantly on my mind as I labored through the pain of my grief. Finally, one day I felt that I had to talk to them. I called Linda and asked to meet with her.

"Why do you do this?" I asked. "Why do you work here in this building where your son died?"

With her beautiful, peaceful smile, Linda answered very simply, "Because it helps me, Dr. Nikaidoh. It helps me to be here."

But I couldn't understand. How could this help her?

I decided to contact Julie Lackey. Julie was no longer working at Children's Medical Center by this time, and her co-workers had lost track of her. The ICU gave me Julie's last known address and phone numbers. I tried every one of them, but she had obviously moved.

I went through every page of Kimberly Lackey's twenty-year-old medical record and tried every single phone number I could find. But none of them worked. So I looked up all the known Julie Lackeys in the entire state of Texas. No luck there, either. I also checked the Texas Nurses Association Directory, but no Julie Lackey was listed. I was ready to do almost anything for the opportunity to speak to Julie. So as a last resort, I went to Restland Funeral Home in the hopes of tracking down visitors of Kimberly's grave. But the funeral home was not able to help me.

When I was just about ready to give up, I found several copies of old bills in Kimberly's file, bills related to her medical care. I had already checked the phone numbers and addresses on these bills, and they hadn't led me anywhere. But this time I noticed that one had a number penciled in on the back—no name, just a number. I tried it and I reached Julie's mother-in-law. Julie called me only a few hours later.

"Julie, I'm so happy to speak to you. I've been looking for you, and I'm so relieved," I said.

"I've been here all along," she answered, "not too far from Children's."

I told her that I thought her decision to go into nursing and then to come back to Children's was unbelievably noble. I told her I wanted to know why she did that. Wasn't it painful for her to work in this profession? And particularly painful to work in the building where Kimberly died?"

"It's not that complicated," she said. "And it's not that noble."

But I disagreed. And I disagree still.

What I eventually learned from Linda, Julie, and the six other women who have so generously shared their stories for this book is that it *is* possible to move beyond the excruciating pain of losing a child. Although there is no end to the period of grieving for a lost child, it is possible to share the joy and light of being alive again. And at least for these eight parents, it is possible to infuse their own lives with a deeper meaning by giving back to the very community that tried valiantly, though unsuccessfully, to save the lives of their precious children.

"I tell you the truth, unless a kernel of wheat falls to the ground and dies, it remains only a single seed. But if it dies, it produces many seeds."

John 12:24
New International Version

The author with Hitoshi (left)

CHAPTER 2

LINDA OJEDA BALCIOGLU

On a bright spring morning in 1983, a small boy was rushed into the Intensive Care Unit at Children's Medical Center in Dallas, surrounded by nurses and emergency medical technicians. A breathing tube had already been inserted into his windpipe, and one of the technicians was squeezing the breathing bag by hand to keep the child alive. Before long, his mother came in and stayed close to his bed, obviously deeply disturbed. But even in her fear, she had an expression of strong determination on her face.

O N THE MORNING OF Raymond's accident, there were four of us at home. My sister and I were visiting and sharing some donuts. My live-in housekeeper, Consuelo, was there, and my two-year-old son, Raymond. My two older children—Liza, eleven, and Ben, ten—were at school.

My husband was not there. About two months before Raymond's accident, my husband had suddenly announced that he didn't want to be married anymore. I was completely shocked by his decision to leave, absolutely devastated. I always loved him, and I always believed he would come back. But that's why he was not there that morning.

My husband and I had a beautiful, two-story, contemporary home, designed perfectly for entertaining—much quieter and sad, though, since he had left. Raymond was still a baby and hadn't been in the pool very much. But the rest of us had spent a lot of time swimming, enjoying our family, our friends, and ourselves. Three rooms in our home had sliding glass doors—with locks, of course—that opened directly onto the pool area. That particular morning, some toys and rafts were floating around in the pool. It never occurred to me at the time, but those toys must have been a very inviting attraction to a naturally curious toddler.

When we finished our coffee and donuts, I told my sister and Consuelo that I was going to take a shower, and I went into the bathroom. After showering, when I came out in my robe, I didn't immediately see Raymond. I asked where he was.

Then I turned around and saw him floating face down in the pool.

I ran outside and jumped in to pull him out. But I didn't know CPR. I didn't know what to do. One of our neighbors, a former military man, must have heard our screams, and he somehow climbed over the fence to come help us. I think he started CPR. Then the paramedics arrived—someone must have called 9-1-1—and took Raymond to Presbyterian Hospital in Dallas. I tried to climb in with him, but they wouldn't let me.

I must have gone back into the house to take off my soaking robe and put some clothes on. Someone must have driven me to the hospital. But I honestly don't remember any of that. All I know is that I was at Presbyterian Hospital hearing someone say, "This is a near drowning."

I was never so happy to hear any single word in my life as I was to hear the word *near* placed next to *drowning*. That meant Raymond was alive. They immediately told us that we had to take him to Children's Medical Center. Again, they wouldn't let me ride in the ambulance, and I had no idea how I got to Children's. But there I was in the ICU.

Someone said to me, "Mrs. Ojeda, we will do our best. We'll do everything we can for him. And we'll just see how he does."

At that point, as a parent, you can't really understand what's happening. You just can't take it in. I just kept thinking, "Raymond is big for a two-year-old. He's so strong. This can't be happening."

All I could really process that day was guilt—the terrible, terrible guilt.

I stayed with Raymond from then on, at his bedside every minute they would allow me there. Otherwise, I was in the ICU waiting room with all the other families. I slept in a recliner, on a couch, whatever I could find. Some of my family members came and went, but I was in a world of my own.

My older two children were not among the visitors. That's because I wouldn't allow it. I wanted to protect Liza and Ben from the pain I was feeling. I didn't want them to be frightened by seeing Raymond in the ICU. So I kept them away, and I only saw them two times when I ran home for a few minutes. I know now what a terrible mistake that was, and I've discussed it with them many times. They were suffering, just as we all were. But their suffering was made worse by the fact that I wouldn't allow them to see their brother. And they were missing me terribly too, when they needed their mother so badly. It was such a terrifying time for all of us. We could have provided comfort for each other. But in an effort to shield them from pain, I closed them out.

My husband did come to the hospital to see his son. In fact, he came many times during the first week or so. After that, I think he lost hope that Raymond would ever really come back, and the whole situation became too painful for him. He visited less and less frequently. It just hurt him too badly to see his son like that.

But for a mom, the hope for recovery never goes away. I

don't care whether a child has tubes and wires coming out from everywhere and is hooked up to every machine possible. I don't care how bad it looks or what the doctors say. No matter what, a mother never loses hope. I know I never did.

During those days and nights in the hospital, the other children and parents in the ICU became my family, and the doctors and nurses too. Because the children were all together in one big open room, if something happened to one child, everyone else felt it. When you're living in the waiting room of the ICU, it's not just your baby. All the children were our babies. We took care of everyone's phone calls, and we shared their sadness, their happiness, and their miracles. We were all in it together—for better and for worse. Without the support of those families, I don't know what I would have done.

Twenty days after his accident, Raymond had never regained consciousness, and his vital signs were steadily worsening. All I wanted was to take him home. If we could just get him home, I knew he would regain consciousness and begin his long healing process. That's all I wanted, and the doctors finally agreed to release him.

The hospital social worker took such good care of me during that time, making sure I had everything ready to bring him home, helping me prepare for that transition. Raymond was on a respirator, and we had to feed him through a tube that had been implanted into his stomach, but I knew I could handle it all. I was ready.

The night before we were scheduled to leave the hospital, May 13, 1983, Raymond passed away.

Looking back now, I truly believe in my heart that God blessed Raymond by taking him at that time. I know those words might be difficult to believe or understand—but they are absolutely the truth. I know other mothers of near-drowning victims whose children have been at home with them for ten years or even fifteen years. During all that time, these children have never regained consciousness. They have never opened their eyes or spoken one word. For all those years, they have been trapped in those bodies. I would never have wanted that for Raymond. Instead, God blessed Raymond by setting him free that night.

At the time, of course, I didn't feel that way. All I knew was that my own life had been taken from me—only worse. I was in the room with Raymond when he passed away, and I would not let anyone else touch him. I pulled out all his intravenous lines and tubes myself. Then I picked him up and held him. I carried my baby in my arms for three hours. I knew the doctors and nurses were watching me, but no one ever told me I had to put my baby down or that it was time for me to go.

When *I* felt it was time, I carefully laid Raymond back on his bed. Then I drove myself home, alone. I do not know how I made it home that night. I have no idea. The doctors were worried about me too. The hospital called to make sure I had arrived home safely.

Then, four weeks after my son's funeral, we suffered another death in our family: My niece was killed in a car accident involving a drunk driver.

By that time, my life felt like nothing but one loss piled on top of another. My marriage, my husband. My baby. My niece. It was nothing but pain. It was nothing but hopelessness. I narrowed my world down to work, tears—and alcohol.

Before our divorce, my husband and I owned four restaurants. They were called Ojeda's, and they were a true Dallas institution. As part of my divorce settlement, I kept one of the restaurants. That's where I worked. And when you own a restaurant, you work every single day. It's like being a prisoner without walls. I was absolutely sick with grief and depression, but I couldn't call in and ask for time off. Who would I call? Myself? Who would solve the problems? Answer the questions?

So somehow, I went to work every day. And maybe it was good for me to get my mind involved in the business, in the daily problems that had to be solved, in the commitment, in the struggles. Because when I wasn't working, I was drinking. Alcohol was the only thing that took away the pain for even a moment. So I drank and I cried. Then I drank some more. If I hadn't had to work, I might have just been drinking the entire day.

During those first years after Raymond's death, I couldn't bear for my children to be away from me. I needed them obsessively. Every single moment that I wasn't at work, I wanted them right next to me—even in bed. Liza slept in the bed with me. Ben didn't want to sleep in the bed, so he slept on the floor in my room. And I did what I could to keep Raymond near me too. I wouldn't let anyone touch his room. I wouldn't allow anyone to touch his clothes, his toys. Everything stayed exactly as it was on the morning of his accident.

For two years, I went on like this. I was depressed, just wracked with pain and guilt, and obsessive and panicked with my children. I knew I was in trouble. But I couldn't seem to figure out another way to live.

Then one day, my mother came in the house and said, "Linda, it's enough. Enough with the kids in the bed. Enough with the drinking. You need to start taking care of yourself! Your children need you. Your family needs you. It's enough. It's time to pull yourself together."

I was in so much pain. But through the fog of my own anguish, I realized that my mother too was in pain—from seeing me like this. I knew she was right. My children did need me. They needed me to be a real mother to them once again. I needed to make a change. So over the next few months, I started taking steps to put my life back together. I went into Raymond's room and opened his closet and drawers. I chose two little pairs of his shoes to keep—and those I will keep forever. Then I began giving his toys and the rest of his shoes and clothes to children who needed them.

I knew I needed to take better care of Liza and Ben—and myself, as well. That's when I decided I could use some additional support. My divorce had become final just after Raymond's death, and I thought it might help me to attend a divorce support group. My church didn't offer one, but I heard that one of the couples who belonged to our church was offering one in their home. I did some research and discovered that the couple was Dr. Nikaidoh and his wife Lynn. I remembered seeing Dr. Nikaidoh every now and then when Raymond was in the ICU. He wasn't Raymond's doctor, so we didn't speak much. But I did remember seeing him there. I decided to join the divorce support group.

About ten people attended each meeting. Pastors and social workers came to speak to us, plus group members shared their own personal stories. Dr. Nikaidoh and Lynn—who had both previously been divorced—were very open with us in sharing some of the bitterness of their own memories and their own family difficulties. From listening to the Nikaidohs and the others in the group, I really began to get a different view of life—one I had never considered before. I started to realize that a failed marriage doesn't mean you're a failure as a person. It doesn't mean that your life is a failure. I began to see that, even though I was divorced, so many wonderful things had come from that marriage: most importantly, my three beautiful children. One child had been ripped away from me in a terrible tragedy. But I still had two beautiful, wonderful gifts from that marriage.

Through my work in the divorce support group, I finally began to realize how much Liza and Ben were suffering and grieving. They had not only lost their brother, but their father had moved to Virginia after the divorce became final. He had been a wonderful provider for his family, but he was not very good at communicating with his children, and he didn't call them as often as they would have liked. And in a way, my children had lost me for a while too. Lost me to the depths of my grief and depression. I could certainly understand why Liza and Ben were angry and hurt.

As I tried to pull my life back together and finally focus on my children's needs, I felt so overwhelmed. It was almost everything I could do to just work at the restaurant and care for Liza and Ben. But there was one additional thing I did make time for: I volunteered in an organization called SPLASH.

SPLASH was a small political advocacy group organized by the doctor who was the head of the ICU at Children's Medical Center where Raymond had been treated. This doctor saw so many babies and young children drown or almost drown every summer. He wanted to influence the state of Texas to adopt laws requiring better fencing around swimming pools, and he encouraged me to become involved. I was glad to do anything I could, to try to keep other parents from having to go through this tragedy. I even went on TV to talk about the issues. Trying to enact these laws made so much sense to me.

But there was a lot of resistance. After all, we were advocating for laws that would tell people what to do in their own backyards. Even though the point of it was to protect children, people didn't like it, and the laws never came into being. Eventually, the organization was dissolved. It was a disappointment, but at least I felt that I had done something to try to help.

In 1990, after having had problems with the restaurant for quite a while, I decided to sell the business. For seven years, I had been grieving. Now I was trying to remember how to be a good parent to Liza and Ben, attempting to put my life back together for their sake, and working so hard every day. I was exhausted, emotionally and physically. So I sold the restaurant.

I honestly didn't do much for one whole year after that. I really just rested and traveled a bit. At the end of that year, I was ready to go back to work, ready to be productive with my life again. And that's when I made a decision: I wanted to work at Children's Medical Center.

Actually, "decision" isn't quite the right word. I can't explain it really. It's just something I knew. I just knew that the only thing that made sense—the only way to move forward with my life—was to work at Children's.

"What is wrong with you?" my mother asked me. "Look what happened to you there. What are you thinking? From the minute you walk into that hospital, you're going to be crying the whole time. You know that. You won't be able help anyone else there. You'll just be crying."

I understood my mother's concerns and why she said what she did. But it wasn't true. I knew I could be helpful there. In my heart, I knew I belonged at Children's. I needed to be there. I just had to be there.

I had met the hospital's director of social work through SPLASH. So I made an appointment to see her and told her I wanted a job. Without even going through a formal interview, she hired me to work in the Hematology/Oncology Department. I was thrilled. But I'll admit that I was a bit nervous too.

On my first day at work, I forced myself to walk into the ICU where Raymond had been cared for. My job was on a different floor, but I knew I had to face the ICU at some time, and I wanted to do it right away. My heart was pounding as I walked down that corridor. The moment I walked into the waiting room area, I felt like crying. But I said some prayers, and I kept telling myself over and over again, "Don't cry. Don't cry. Don't cry. Don't cry." Somehow, I made it through.

From the ICU, I went back up to the floor I would be working on and knew right then that I would be fine at the hospital. In fact, I absolutely loved my job.

I started out in Hematology patient relations—registering the families who came in for treatment of blood cancers, putting in their lab work. From the very beginning, it felt wonderful being there. I loved feeling helpful, knowing that my smile was making a difference for just a moment in the lives of those families. For a while, I was transferred to work in the Admitting Department. I enjoyed the Hematology Department more, but I was happy to serve wherever I was needed—and eventually, I was transferred back to Hematology.

One time, there was a disagreement among some of the staff in our department. Some of my co-workers were angry and asked me if I were angry too. But in my own mind, I was very clear. "I'm here for only one reason. I'm here for the children and the families. I'm here to help the kids. And however I can be helpful, I will be," I explained. "Other than that, I'm not really interested in who blames someone for something. I'm not going to get upset."

That's just the way I am. I don't get angry. I get sad, but I don't get angry. One time during my divorce, my lawyer said to me, "Linda, you need to get angry about this. We need to start a little fire under you to push you forward. Come on, get a little angry."

But that's just not me. My family still teases me about it—especially my children. I might look perfectly calm on the outside to everyone else, but my children will say, "Oh, look at her, she's getting angry. See that little look on her face? That's it. That's Mom being angry. That's as angry as she gets."

Even right after Raymond died, people would ask why I wasn't angry. "What did you do to deserve this?" they would ask. "Why would God do this to you? Aren't you angry?"

I guess that was the way *they* looked at it, but not me. I believe that sometimes things happen for reasons that we cannot understand. Even in the case of terrible, painful tragedy. And there's no point in being angry about it.

After Raymond's death, I wasn't angry at myself for taking a shower that morning. I wasn't angry at my sister. I wasn't angry at Consuelo. We need other people for love, not for anger. In fact, after the accident, Consuelo went back to Mexico, and I never heard from her again. After all these years, I still hope she'll call me one day so I can tell her that I'm not angry. I wish she would call so that we could comfort each other. Comfort serves a purpose. Anger does not.

As it turned out, the experiences I had in Admitting during the short time I was away from Hematology became a turning point that would lead me to a new, and very important, direction in my life. While I was there, I noticed so many Spanish-speaking parents crying with frustration because no one could help them understand what was happening to their children. They had no translators, no interpreters. They might try to find a Spanish speaker in Housekeeping, or they would ask other friends or other patients to translate for them. Sometimes it worked out all right. But sometimes it didn't. Sometimes the person doing the translation didn't really know the appropriate vocabulary or the medical terms. Sometimes they didn't understand the subtleties or how to communicate the tone behind what the doctor was saying. They tried, but they were not always able to fully convey what was being said.

So I spoke to my boss in Admitting, and she allowed me to go translate for some of those families. As a Latina and as a former parent in the hospital, I knew what these parents needed, and I knew the respect they deserved.

From the first time I began translating for these families, I had every confidence that I was the best possible person to help them in their time of crisis. This was the work I was meant to do. This was the work God wanted me to do. I could tell it in my heart. For those many years after Raymond died, I couldn't imagine any sense of purpose in my life beyond my family. But as soon as I began translating, I knew *this* was my purpose.

Before too long, no matter which department I was officially working in, I began keeping my own calendar of appointments for translation services.

I loved helping those families, and I was good at it. From my background in the restaurant business, I knew all about customer service. From the experience of my own personal tragedy, I truly knew what they were going through. I had so much respect for these parents, and it showed. I knew how difficult it was to understand what was happening around you—even *without* a language barrier. So I knew when the parents had reached the limit of information they could take in.

For example, if a child had been in an accident, and the doctor was explaining the situation to the parents, sometimes I had to say to the doctor, "The parents aren't hearing it any more. They can't take in any more information. Why don't we stop for a while and come back to it later?"

At other times, the doctors might have needed permission from the parents to operate on their child—and they needed that permission immediately. I was always able to sit calmly with the parents and talk them through the forms, explaining what it all meant. I was patient with them because I remembered what it was like to be in their position. Consequently, I was the one who was able to get them to sign the forms when others could not. If there were any medical terms I did not know how to translate, I asked for help until I understood. I also studied on my own so I could increase my medical vocabulary.

In the mid-1990s, Children's Medical Center of Dallas established a Translation Department, and I was the first employee—"the pioneer," as my director still calls me. Today, we have almost fifty people working in the hospital as Spanish translators, in addition to "language lines" for other languages.

These days, I work full time as a translator in the Emergency Room—very specialized work at a time when a family is in a terrible crisis. I usually translate for twenty to thirty families each day—sometimes more. I love my work, and I know that what I do is so important for so many people.

I'm not a doctor, a nurse, or a social worker. I'm not there to tell anyone what to do or to guide them in solving their problems. And as difficult as it is sometimes, I'm not there to become friends with the parents, to be advocates for their children, or even to offer my own personal support, no matter what I'm feeling. I am there simply to act as a highway for communication— to help the hospital communicate effectively with the families of the children who have been brought in to their care, and to help the families get the information they need from the hospital personnel.

Doing my job well means that I translate exactly what I hear—the words, the tone, the mood—and that I, myself, am almost invisible. For example, if a mother says to a doctor, "Will my child walk again?" that's exactly what I say too. I don't speak about the mother in the third person. I don't say, "*She* wants to know if *her* child will walk again." As much as possible, I try to speak as the mother. In fact, whenever I can, I try to stand behind the parents, not between them and the doctor. That way, the doctor and the parents have the best possible chance to speak directly to each other as if there were no language barrier at all. I want them to forget that I am even in the room.

Sometimes the work I do is very stressful. But I'm very strong, and I can handle it. I'm even stronger when I'm under the most pressure. There are times when I have to get on the phone and tell a family some very bad news. Maybe their child was in an accident in Dallas, but the family doesn't even live here. Or maybe the doctor needs to know if the family has signed a "do not resuscitate" order. I just have to respond to exactly what the doctor needs. Sometimes I say to the parent, "In all due respect, sir, I am sorry I have to ask you this, but . . ." Whatever the doctor needs the parent to know, I have to say it.

When I am translating, everything I hear and everything I say is completely private. I don't share the information with anyone, not my co-workers, not my friends, not my family. It's as if I never heard it. If I translate for a family and then see them in the hallway at another time, I might nod to them as a sign of recognition and respect. But I won't ever ask them about how their child is doing or about any of the other personal information I might have heard when I was working on their behalf.

It's not that I don't care about their child's situation. It's just that I show my respect for their privacy by not intruding into their lives. What they are going through is so private. They don't need me to be their friend. If their child is ill, they don't need pity from someone they just met. They don't need strangers to judge them.

I've been there, and I know.

In fact, I've kept my own life private too. The people I worked with when I first came to Children's knew about Raymond because I had been on TV with SPLASH. But no one else at the hospital knows. I have never said anything to anyone—even when I've actually worked in the room where Raymond was cared for. I don't want people to know about my own tragedy. That is personal to me. I want to be at the hospital to serve, not for people to feel sorry for me.

The phrase I use to describe my life now is one that I learned from my children. It's what they call "all good." I have been married for the past seven years to a kind and wonderful man, and we share a beautiful life together. I am blessed with wonderful children and grandchildren who are the magic of my life. My children and I have done a lot of talking and repairing of our realtionships. I made a lot of mistakes. I just didn't realize it. But we are "all good" now. I want to be the best person I can be, to set the best example that I can for my husband, children, and grandkids.

I don't look back a lot. I have to let go of anger and try to make everything as peaceful as I can. I've really taken the word "hate" out of my vocabulary. The way I look at it, it takes too much energy to get angry and then get happy again. You feel so awful inside. It's much better just to stay peaceful, just to stay happy. That's how I like to live my life.

My faith—the faith my parents gave me—has been my guide all along. No matter how hard it is to believe, at certain painful times in life, God will always give you a plan. And when you discover the peace of that plan, you will feel free.

I came back to this hospital because it helps me to be here. It helps me to be a better human being. There is so much love and happiness here, even at a place where tragedies are also occurring. I know how much a kind word, a caring smile meant to me when my own world was falling apart. Now, I have a smile on my face every single day, knowing that I'm making a difference in so many lives, helping so many people. I plan to stay here forever.

The righteous cry out, and the Lord hears them; he delivers them from all their troubles. The Lord is close to the brokenhearted and saves those who are crushed in spirit. A righteous man may have many troubles, but the Lord delivers him from them all.

Psalm 34:17–19
New International Version

Linda and Raymond

CHAPTER 3

JULIE LACKEY WILLIAMS

On March 30, 1982, Julie Lackey gave birth to a wonderful blond baby named Kimberly. Kimberly seemed perfect at birth—beautifully formed with all her fingers and toes, pink, seemingly healthy—everything Julie and her husband Danny could have hoped for.

Then, in the blink of an eye, everything changed.

Kimberly began having difficulty breathing, her skin started losing its color, and the doctors whisked her away to the nursery. Within hours, she arrived at Children's Medical Center of Dallas, accompanied by Danny and his family.

I WAS A FIRST-TIME MOM, young—all of twenty-one years old—and the only thing I really understood that day was that something was very wrong. My baby had been taken from me, and soon after, my husband had gone with her. Everything happened so quickly. One minute she was just fine; the next minute she was fighting for her life.

While I was still in another hospital recuperating from childbirth, the doctors at Children's Medical Center examined Kimberly and then explained to Danny that she had been born with two heart defects. First, she had what they called "transposition of the great arteries." That means that the two major arteries that take blood away from the heart were mixed up. So the artery that was supposed to send blood to the lungs, where it would pick up much needed oxygen, was sending that blood out to the body instead. And the artery that was supposed to send highly oxygenated blood out to the body was sending that blood right back to the lungs. Because of this "mix up," her organs and other body tissues just couldn't get the oxygen they needed. Kimberly also had another problem that is common in children with transposition of the great arteries. This is called "ventricular septal defect," a hole between the heart's two lower chambers.

It was a grim situation.

But there was also some good news. Once Kimberly reached thirteen pounds, they could perform a surgery that could bring her long-term stability. To allow Kimberly the chance to survive until she weighed enough for surgery, the cardiologist enlarged the hole between the two upper chambers of the heart. This hole is a natural opening that usually closes within the first few days of life as the baby begins to use her lungs. But in Kimberly's case, we needed it to stay open to increase the amount of oxygen Kimberly's heart would pump out to her body.

Danny came back to me later in the day, bringing a hand-drawn sketch of Kimberly's heart problems—and a lock of her precious blond hair. The doctors did the procedure to enlarge the hole in her heart's upper chambers, and it was successful. We brought Kimberly home when she was five days old.

Because Kimberly was my first child and I had so little experience, I just didn't fully realize how sick she was. For example, she had such a weak cry that we never heard her waking up. The dog would start barking, and that's how we'd know she was awake. But since that was the norm for us, we didn't realize that her tiny little cry was a sign of her heart problem. Maybe that was a blessing. We were just able to love and enjoy her for who she was, without spending all our time constantly worrying. Our immediate goal for Kimberly was to put some weight on her. We had to get her up to that thirteen-pound mark. Consequently, bottle-feeding became our constant, all-day challenge. Since she didn't have as much oxygen as a healthy baby, sucking was extraordinarily hard work for her, even though we used the preemie nipples. In fact, if she sucked for too long, she would start to turn blue. So it was a real struggle just to get a couple of ounces down. Then, her gut couldn't digest it well— again due to lack of oxygen supply. So most of her hard-won formula came right back up again. It seemed like a never-ending battle. But she couldn't have that life-saving surgery until we got her weight up. So we just kept at it all the time.

It took us almost nine months to get her weight up to thirteen pounds. But we did it.

Kimberly's surgery—called the Mustard procedure—was scheduled for December, and we could hardly wait. From what we understood, this surgery would give Kimberly a good, fighting chance at a pretty normal life. We knew she would probably need additional surgery at some point in the future, maybe as an adolescent, and that her activities might need to be somewhat restricted. But we also knew that the Mustard procedure would enable her to eat well, digest her food, grow, and thrive in a way that she had not yet been able to do. We were very anxious to get this surgery done.

But when we brought Kimberly in to the hospital, the doctors discovered she had an ear infection. The surgery had to be postponed. Dr. Nikaidoh explained that they just couldn't subject her to surgery with an infection already in her body. But we could tell he was concerned about the postponement. Kimberly had abnormally high blood pressure in her pulmonary artery— the artery that sends blood to the lungs for oxygenation—and that was a dangerous condition. But we had no choice. We absolutely had to wait until her ear infection cleared up.

By the second week of January 1983, Dr. Nikaidoh said he

could go ahead with the surgery. At that time, they did the Mustard operation and also closed the ventricular septal defect that she was born with. The hope was that these two operations together would bring more oxygen to all parts of Kimberly's body and also lower the high blood pressure in her pulmonary artery.

The surgery went well. But as the day went on, Kimberly had a lot of bleeding in her chest, and they took her back to the operating room. Luckily, they were able to control the bleeding. Since she'd had two major surgeries in one day, they decided to put her on a ventilator to give her some respiratory support.

After her surgeries, Kimberly was the most beautiful pink baby, and we were thrilled. As far as we knew, the only problem was the fact that she needed to stay on the ventilator. They tried taking her off it twice, but she just would not start breathing on her own. So Kimberly stayed in the hospital for three months on the ventilator.

During those three months, this baby absolutely became the belle of the ball. The nurses all loved her, and she just ate up the attention. One day when we went in, we discovered that one of the local high schools had donated blood on her behalf. Another time, she was dressed and sitting up in her bed wearing sunglasses in the shape of stars. Everyone loved Kimberly.

Because of her age—less than a year old—and because our time with her had been restricted immediately after her surgery, Kimberly began to relate to her caregivers as her family. It was such an important time in her life for bonding, and she was getting to know the staff at Children's better than she knew us. So after being in the ICU for about ten weeks, she was moved into a private room, and we moved in with her. Because of the ventilator, we were required to have a private-duty nurse with us too. But still, we had Kimberly more to ourselves, and she was getting a chance to know us as her family.

About a week before her first birthday, we started learning how to care for Kimberly on the ventilator so we could take her home. But the nurses decided to try one more time to see if she could breathe on her own—and she did fine! Just in time for her first birthday, we were able to take our little girl home by herself, without machines. Danny and I were so thrilled.

The next couple of years were wonderful for us, really a blessing. Kimberly ate well, grew, and developed normally—walking and talking non-stop with no developmental delays. Other than a couple of medications she took on a daily basis, she didn't even require any special care. We did go to Children's for a check-up about every three months, and the reports were generally good, although the doctors did share their concern about her continued elevated blood pressure in the pulmonary artery. Danny and I weren't too worried about it. We figured there would be some way to get that down.

So in general, our lives were pretty normal. I worked on an electronics assembly line, and my husband worked at Texas Instruments. Kimberly went to day care, and when she was about two and a half, our son Brian was born—perfectly healthy. Kimberly absolutely loved mothering him and bossing him around. She called him her "Bubba."

Both of the kids were healthy and doing great—except that Brian came down with the chicken pox in infancy and, of course, Kimberly caught it from him. They both had very mild cases, maybe only about ten spots on each of them, and I didn't worry about it any more than any other mom would have. Overall, we were feeling pretty normal.

In mid-February of 1986, just before Kimberly's third birthday, we went to Children's for our regularly scheduled visit. They examined Kimberly and took a chest x-ray and a sonogram. A few days later, they asked us to come back to the hospital to conference with the doctor. Kimberly had been doing fine, so I wasn't sure why they wanted to see me. Nevertheless, Danny was working, so I took both children and went to meet Kimberly's cardiologist. It was the day of my twenty-fifth birthday.

That's when the doctor told me Kimberly had about six months to live.

The tests showed that Kimberly's heart muscle had signifi-cantly weakened, and the failing heart was causing a rise in blood pressure in her pulmonary artery. It was possible that her heart had been weakened by the chicken pox. Or maybe her artery was damaged while we had waited for her ear infection to clear up. But the truth is, we'll never know. And whatever the cause, there was now a constant struggle going on in Kimberly's heart and lungs: too much pressure in the blood vessels of the lungs, which was burdening the weakened heart.

The doctors at Children's could offer no medications or surgery to help her. But before we accepted her inevitable death, they encouraged us to at least look at one other option, her only option: a heart–lung transplant. Although it wasn't performed at Children's, five other medical centers in the U.S. did perform heart–lung transplants on children.

We knew the doctors didn't really hold out much hope, but they sent Kimberly's medical records to all five. Three of the centers never responded. But the doctors did hear back from two. Texas Children's Hospital said no, they would not consider Kimberly for the surgery. But the Medical Center of Virginia said yes, they would consider her as a heart–lung transplant candidate. However, they pointed out that the procedure was considered experimental. They put Kimberly's chance of survival at only two percent.

Danny and I had to make a terrible decision. The doctors gave us all the information they could, but the decision itself was ours. Finally, we chose to focus on Kimberly's quality of life. We decided to let her grow up, best as she could, without putting her through such arduous surgery for probably no good outcome. She was a strong-willed child, and we felt she had a lot left to do in this life. Some of our family members thought— and still think—we made the wrong call on that. They feel we should have put her through the transplant, even for just a two-percent chance. But Danny and I were sure about our decision. We knew it was best for Kimberly.

Once we made our decision against the heart–lung transplant, we had to accept the news that Kimberly only had a few months to live. But how do you accept news like that? How do you make sense of it? What do you do?

What I did was quit my job. I wanted to be home to make sure she rested well and didn't exhaust herself. But more importantly, I wanted to spend every moment with Kimberly that I possibly could. And we applied to the Make-A-Wish Foundation. They graciously helped Kimberly's Disney World dream come true. The four of us went while Kimberly still had the energy, and we had a wonderful time.

When we got back home, I was nervous and watchful over everything she did. I'll admit that I did hover a bit—probably more than a bit—and she let me know that she didn't like it. Never a shy one and always wise beyond her years, Kimberly looked at me one day about four months after I'd quit my job.

"Mom," she said simply, "go back to work. Please."

It was my instinct to hover. I couldn't really help myself. But Kimberly didn't like it. In addition, I knew I had to learn to let go, little by little. Kimberly was only three, but she deserved a chance to develop and grow and explore for whatever time she had left on this earth—without me hanging over her shoulder and asking every fifteen seconds if she was tired.

So, I did go back to work. I went back to the same company, although I had to take a different job. Instead of working on the assembly line, I worked as a secretary. And as my precocious daughter told me, she and her brother were very happy to go back to day care.

Before we knew it, six months had gone by. Kimberly was holding her own, and so we relaxed a bit. We didn't pretend to ourselves that she would get well. We knew we were going to lose her, but we were grateful to have a little bit more time than we had feared.

Kimberly knew she was very ill. We tried to be honest with her, as we felt it was appropriate. We talked to her about heaven and what it's like for people when they die. And she interpreted what we said in her own way, based on her own frame of reference.

One day, we were all getting dressed to go to a wedding.

Kimberly came out of her room dressed in a frilly dress. On her feet, she wore her favorite Punky Brewster™ multicolored tennis shoes: yellow, turquoise, orange, and pink. "You need to go change those shoes," I told her. "You can't wear tennis shoes to the wedding."

Kimberly put her hands on her hips and said to me, "I want you to know that when I get to heaven, Jesus has a very big closet. And He does *not* care what you wear with Punky Brewster tennis shoes!"

I took a breath. "Well," I said, "I am not Jesus, and this is not heaven. Go change your shoes."

It was all I could do to keep from crying. But that was Kimberly—sassy with a lot more wisdom than children her age should have. Always curious, always thinking things through in her own way.

For the next couple of years, we were in and out of the hospital quite often. Kimberly would become lethargic, swollen, and complain that her chest hurt. Those were the symptoms of congestive heart failure caused by the problems with her heart and lungs. We would bring her in to Children's, and they would give her some morphine drips, drain fluid from her lungs, and give some medication for her heart. After a few days, we'd go home again. For a while, Kimberly would have more energy and feel a bit better.

Even during those hospital visits, Kimberly's personality was out in full force. In fact, she was famous in the hospital for keeping a particular toy under the covers with her—a plastic ice-cream cone with a foam ball on top—and "surprising" doctors by shooting it at them when they bent down to listen to her chest. Dr. Nikaidoh and the other doctors were such good sports. Somehow, they just always seemed to "fall" for that! And Kimberly's laughter when she popped that ball out at them was always a welcome bit of sunshine.

It was during this time, we found out later, that Dr. Nikaidoh tried to help us by purchasing a drug for Kimberly in Mexico. He had gone down to San Louis Potosi in order to assist a doctor with several pediatric heart surgeries. At the time, there was a medication called oral amrinone that he thought would help to both strengthen Kimberly's heart and relax her pulmonary artery, lowering the pressure in it. It was available in Europe but not in the U.S. Dr. Nikaidoh did everything he could to try to get it in Mexico, but he just couldn't find it.

When he flew back from San Louis Potosi, the U.S. Customs officer who opened his attaché case noticed his stethoscope and asked him if he had purchased any medicine in Mexico. Dr. Nikaidoh said he had not. Had he found the medicine he was looking for, it would have been illegal for him to bring it into the U.S. since it wasn't approved for use here, and he would have been in serious trouble if he'd been caught with it at the border. But he told us that if he had been able to find the medicine she needed, he would have taken that risk for Kimberly without hesitation. That's the kind of care we had at Children's. It was extraordinary.

Throughout all the hospitalizations, the fatigue and the discomfort of those few years, this little girl had one main goal in life: Kimberly Lackey wanted to go to kindergarten. She talked about it all the time. She planned for it all the time. She was always playing school and teaching her classmates at daycare the numbers and letters. Kimberly knew she had to be five years old in order to go—and she also knew she didn't have quite as much time left on this earth as most other children her age.

All she wanted to do was make it to kindergarten, so that became my goal as well.

And we made it. In September 1987, Kimberly entered kindergarten with all the other children—just as she wanted. We have a wonderful picture of her from that first day with her purple backpack, Punky Brewster tennis shoes, her beautiful blond hair, and a big gorgeous smile. She had made her goal, and she was so proud. I too will always be so proud of that accomplishment and Kimberly's tenacity to fulfill her dreams.

Then, in my heart, I believe that having attained that goal, she was ready to let go. She had fulfilled her mission. After only two weeks, Kimberly became too fatigued to continue. The school district sent us a tutor, and we did some home schooling for a while.

During this last year of Kimberly's life, we were in the hospital every three to four weeks, draining the fluid that had built up and trying to keep her comfortable. She knew she wasn't going to live much longer, and we tried to answer her questions as honestly as we could. She had a friend at the hospital, a little girl who was a couple of years older than Kimberly was. This child had also been in and out of the hospital for many years. They both knew they were probably not going to be in this world too much longer. And I can honestly say there is nothing more humbling than walking in on two children talking about their deaths.

Kimberly understood as much as she could about the situation, and sometimes she seemed to know more than we did. One time when we were in the hospital and she was in congestive heart failure, the doctors told us to call our family. Danny and I made the calls and brought everyone in to her little cramped room.

All of a sudden, Kimberly sat up, looked around, and said, "Why are you all here? Go home. I'm not going anywhere today." And she was right.

And when it *was* time, Kimberly seemed to know that too.

In May 1988, we had been in the hospital for almost three weeks. The doctors allowed us to go home for the weekend with the understanding that we would come back on Monday. We had a great weekend, but Kimberly seemed pensive, as if she had a lot on her mind. At the end of the weekend, Kimberly told me she wanted to give her grandmother the tape back that she had borrowed. This was Barbra Streisand doing "Who's Afraid of the Big Bad Wolf?" that Kimberly had listened to over and over and over.

"Why do you want to give the tape back?" I asked her.

"I won't be needing it anymore," she said. "I'm going to go to heaven."

On Monday, when it was time to go back to the hospital, she

brought all her favorite stuffed animals with her. And she gave them out to the nurses, one at a time.

On Wednesday, she became very lethargic. She told Danny, "Daddy, you don't need to go to work today."

Kimberly colored me a picture, and then she went into a deep sleep. A few of my friends came in from Heart to Heart, a support group for heart parents. They had brought her a balloon she had asked for and a new Sleeping Beauty™ nightgown as a gift. Kimberly woke up to put on the gown. Then she said her chest was hurting, so I walked out of the room to get a nurse while her daddy stayed by her side.

While I was down the hall, Kimberly died.

She was lying on her bed, surrounded by family and friends, wearing her Sleeping Beauty nightgown. In my heart, I believe Kimberly orchestrated her death as she had lived her life—on her own terms. As Frank Sinatra's song states, "she did it her way."

Although we knew Kimberly was going to die, I'm not sure that knowledge made it any easier. She was so full of life, brought so much joy to all of us, and had touched so many lives in her short time on earth. I could not believe that she was actually gone. The loss was devastating.

I guess Danny, Brian, and I coped as well as we could with the loss. We knew it would take a while for us to feel like a family again without her. We just went through the motions of getting through the days.

Two months later, we were still reeling from the shock of losing Kimberly—emotionally drained and just exhausted—when Danny started to feel sick. He ended up with a fever and congestion. Danny was a weight lifter, a big strong man who didn't "cry uncle" very easily. But when he began spitting up blood, he knew he needed to go to the doctor. They admitted him immediately to a local hospital where they discovered he had pneumonia. In order to treat him effectively, the doctor needed to do a bronchoscopy to determine the exact type of pneumonia. After that procedure, they decided to put him on a ventilator for a short while to help him recover.

I was sitting out in the ICU waiting room, wondering how soon Danny could come home, when a nurse came out to find me.

"Mrs. Lackey?"

"Yes."

"Mrs. Lackey, we've lost your husband."

"Well, he's here somewhere. He's a really big guy, and he didn't just disappear," I said. I was exhausted and impatient. "I'm sure you can find out where they've taken him."

"No," she said. "We lost him. He's dead." She turned around and walked away.

And that was it.

I had expected Kimberly's death. But Danny's death—in such a cold, uncaring environment—was almost more than I could bear. Suddenly, Brian and I were all that was left of our family. I don't know how I made it through Danny's funeral and the following weeks. My life was just a blur of pain.

Although my primary goal was to try to keep things as "normal" for Brian as possible, I felt that we just couldn't continue in our house. There were just too many memories. So I sold the house, and Brian and I moved to a different suburb of Dallas.

Everything was so difficult for Brian. He had suffered so much, so many losses, and he was angry to be so different from the other children.

Even at four years old, he would ask, "Why did this have to happen to us? Why can't I have a father and a sister like everyone else?"

It was hard to find answers that would comfort him. I understood his questions and the depth of his pain—and the fact that no answers would bring his family back. The truth is that I was so busy trying to take care of Brian and trying to make things as good as possible for him, that I don't think I really grieved for Danny or Kimberly for years. I was in emotional shock. With the support of my family, it was all I could do to keep myself together and going through the days.

My friends tried to be helpful too. They listened to me when I needed to talk, and they would watch Brian if I needed a break. But their support was really limited. Most of them were in their twenties, as was I. We were all so young. Many were single and had no children. They simply had no way to understand what I was going through. In fact, some friends talked about my losses almost as if they were simply a bump in the road of my life.

"You're so young," they'd say. "You need to move on. After all, you have your whole life in front of you."

I couldn't seem to explain it to them. My child was dead. My husband was dead. The life I had known—the life I thought I would have, the family I thought I would have—was over. It was behind me. At that time, I couldn't visualize the "whole life" they saw in front of me. Maybe they saw it. But I didn't.

Sadly, things were awkward even with my friends who did have children. Once I was invited to a birthday party for a friend's daughter—but I just could not go. This little girl had blonde hair and blue eyes just like Kimberly. And I couldn't face the pain of going to a store to buy a gift for a little girl Kimberly's age. It was just too much for me. I tried to explain it to my friend, and she said she understood. But after that, she was always very guarded when she spoke about her girls. I know she was probably just trying to make sure I didn't feel bad, but our friendship was never as relaxed and as candid as it was before the birthday party.

I struggled along for a while, best as I could, just working and trying to focus on Brian. Then one day, I got a phone call from a young man I had dated before marrying Danny. I'll call him "Thomas."

After a while, Thomas and I started dating again. To be honest, it felt good to have someone else in my life, to have another adult to share things with. Since Danny's death, I had kept myself emotionally very guarded, not letting anyone come too close. But with Thomas, I eventually let my guard down.

As it turned out, I let my guard down for the wrong reasons and with the wrong person. Thomas was a very controlling young man. But I was so vulnerable at that time; I was incapable of seeing the big picture. I dated him for a long time without being able to see how unhealthy the relationship was.

Thomas had very strong opinions about grief and how I should deal with my losses. I tried to understand and accept his opinions—because that's what he wanted—but it was very difficult. He believed I should not have any pictures of Kimberly in my house. He didn't even want me to talk about the life I had before we started dating. He told me all the time that I just needed to forget what had happened and move on. Thomas had lost his father at a very young age, and his mother had never spoken of him again. Maybe that's how Thomas thought people should deal with their grief. And maybe that's okay for some people. I don't know. But it was not right for me.

After dating for five years, Thomas asked me to marry him, and I said "yes." It seemed like the thing I should do. Thankfully, however, I came to my senses about the relationship before we went through with the wedding. When I finally realized that Thomas was controlling and not a good role model for Brian, I broke off the engagement.

Thomas was enraged by my decision and responded by hurting me the deepest way he knew how. He took my only copy of my favorite picture of Kimberly—the very last photograph taken of her before she died. I am so grateful that my parents had a copy of that picture. And now I also have one.

It was during my relationship with Thomas that I finally starting grieving for Kimberly and for Danny. I finally let myself experience the full pain of my losses. With the help of a counselor, I progressed through the five stages of grieving that Dr. Elizabeth Kubler-Ross brought out in her book *On Death and Dying*: denial, anger, bargaining, depression, and acceptance. I don't think every person necessarily goes through these exact steps in this order. But for me, I had been working so hard to keep things together for Brian that I hadn't even allowed myself to *begin* the grieving process until years after Danny's death. It felt good to finally put some closure to the feelings I had kept bottled up for so long.

Around the time of my thirtieth birthday, I started to take serious stock of where I wanted to go with my life. At that time, I was working as an administrative assistant for six executives in a company that made environmental control systems. I began to realize that I could never make a decent living for Brian and myself in that job. I had to find something different to do.

One of my grandmothers had been a nurse, and I had always been interested in nursing. But more importantly, Kimberly inspired me in that direction. She inspired me to be all that I could be. I wanted to be in a position to give back some of the love and care that had come our way during Kimberly's illness. I wanted to be the type of nurse who knows what it's like to be on the receiving end of that care, who knows how absolutely important it is.

Once I made up my mind, I went to see my boss and told him I was quitting. I told him what my plans were, and he was so incredibly kind. He asked me if I knew which school I was going to and if I were familiar with the enrollment process. I had to admit to him that I didn't know anything about it—only that it would be really difficult.

At lunchtime that day, he came by my desk. "Julie, get your purse," he said. "We're going on a field trip."

My boss drove me to Texas Woman's University in Denton, about twenty-five miles north of Dallas. We met with the Dean of Physical Therapy, who was a friend of his wife. After speaking with her, we went to the admissions office, where I was given the applications and requirements for admission. He even helped me sign up for the SAT college entrance exam.

I will never forget his kindness.

I flourished and excelled in nursing school. The first two years were difficult because the students were mostly young and not easy for me to relate to. But once I began my junior year— the actual beginning of nursing classes—I met students of all ages and backgrounds. I made fast friends, including some who are still close friends today.

It was incredibly hard work, but I knew it was exactly where I needed to be. I loved the classes in nursing theory as well as the clinical rotations. I loved the way the patients accepted our help as we learned to write individualized care plans. And although it was emotionally difficult for me when I knew a patient was going to die, I found that I could be a great support to the families since I could relate to their emotions and impending loss. I'm not sure one person can ever fully understand another person's feelings, but you can offer valuable empathy from having walked that same road before. And as I helped others work with their grief as a student nurse, I learned once again that "normal" includes a wide range of behaviors and feelings. I learned how to meet others wherever they are in their own grief process, and I learned how critical that is to good and successful grieving—which eventually allows a person to truly move on in life.

Toward the end of my nursing studies, one of my clinical rotations was at Children's Medical Center on the fourth floor, exactly where Kimberly had been cared for. My professors talked to me at length about whether or not I would really be able to do it. It was tough, very tough, but I knew I had to do it. I walked up there with my classmates.

Being on that floor brought on a strong sense of déjà vu. I had spent so much of my life right there. And many of the same nurses who had helped Kimberly were there—surprised to see me but welcoming me this time as a member of their team. They all seemed happy that I'd chosen nursing as a career and were wonderful mentors as I learned to write care plans, administer medications, and understand the disease process of the patient I was assigned. They were all so supportive and kind.

I also crossed paths with Dr. Nikaidoh on the floor, and it was wonderful to see him again. He was happy to see me, but not terribly surprised that I had gone into nursing. He told me that at Danny's funeral, I had mentioned to him that I might become a nurse. I honestly don't remember that. But then again, I don't remember too much from that time.

I graduated from nursing school in 1994 and immediately

began working at Children's Medical Center in the Intensive Care Unit. I chose the ICU because I wanted an environment where I could care for only one or two patients at a time in a more thorough manner instead of the six or eight patients I would have had out on the floor. I chose Children's in particular because I was familiar with the high standards of care and because I wanted to give back to the institution that had done so much for Kimberly and our family.

Most of my patients were cardiac patients. (Today, the hospital has a separate Cardiac ICU.) I even took care of one little boy who had transposition of the great arteries, the condition Kimberly had. He had the surgery to switch the arteries and was very sick for several weeks. His parents were so young. I was able to bond with the family and help them understand his setbacks and celebrate his small victories toward recovery.

But the truth is that working at Children's was extremely stressful and difficult for me emotionally. I found that I couldn't really leave my job when I went home; I constantly thought about my patients and their families. I wasn't able to handle my emotions well when my patient died—especially a cardiac patient. And there had been so many improvements in cardiac care since Kimberly had been sick that I found myself focusing over and over again on "what if . . . what if."

I realized I needed some help, and I spoke with my nurse manager. She arranged for me to have fewer cardiac cases.

Still, for the next six months, I struggled. I did *not* know what to do. It was so painful for me to be there. But I had made a commitment, and I didn't want to let anyone down. I was particularly disturbed by the thought of disappointing the nurses who had cared for Kimberly, interviewed me for the job at Children's, and recommended me for employment!

Sometime later, Dr. Nikaidoh told me that he'd been concerned when he saw me on staff there in the ICU. After all, he said, it had only been six years since Kimberly had died there. He was right. Although I didn't realize it at the time, I was really grieving during the year I worked at Children's. I had wanted to work there to give back to the place that had done so much for my daughter. I wanted to work with the doctors and nurses that never, ever gave up on Kimberly and gave so much to our family over and over. I knew this hospital would be a place where I could really make a difference; as a nurse, I knew what the children needed, and as Kimberly's mom, I knew what the parents needed.

Nevertheless, I was burning out way too quickly in the ICU. I finally realized I needed to leave. It was a painful and difficult decision, but it was the right one for me.

Although my year at Children's was very difficult, something wonderful also happened during that time: I started doing weekend home visits for some children. I found that I loved it. I loved seeing the physical and emotional environment they lived in, instead of only seeing them in the artificiality of the hospital. Seeing them in their homes helped me to provide much better care. I loved the one-to-one interaction with the patient and parents, and I was able to see how the instructions for care written in the hospital translated to home. How did the medication schedule, doctor appointments, therapy, etc. fit into the home environment? How did the child thrive at home, given both the child's limitations and the family's individual dynamic? Those weren't questions you could answer by providing care only in the hospital.

From my own experience with Kimberly, I knew how difficult it could be to come home from the hospital with a baby who wasn't well. Cardiac children like Kimberly often have difficulty eating and keeping their nourishment down. But hospitals don't always give practical tips—like using a preemie nipple or adding cereal to breast milk or formula for added nutrition. A nurse in the home can also help parents better manage medication schedules that are conducive to the family's sleep and wake schedules, as well as daycare or school.

So when I left Children's, I transitioned into home care. At one job, I was also asked to write a grant application for Ryan White Funds for infusion medications for HIV patients. I ended up providing home infusion therapy—that is, giving intravenous drugs in the home—for a lot of children and adults with HIV. I truly enjoyed the journey these patients were walking. I understood where they were coming from. So many of the young men were gay, had been disowned by their families, and had little support. I was glad they now had someone who cared, someone they could rely on when needed. I was glad to be the person who could just sit and talk with them about what they had done in their lives, their accomplishments and regrets, the way their disease ravaged their bodies and minds—whatever they needed to discuss.

I knew that many of my patients did not have long to stay on this earth. While some people might have found that difficult or depressing, I loved every minute of it. I was finally at a place in my own life and my own grieving process where I could help others have a meaningful end-of-life experience. I truly believe that all people have something specific to accomplish and complete on this earth. Kimberly taught me that. So it's such an honor for me to walk with people through that journey, caring for them as they pull the pieces of their lives together in a meaningful manner.

I now work for a nationwide company that establishes infusion suites—specialized offices where patients can come just for chemotherapy or other IV medications. I travel a lot to help open suites around the country. That's the business part of it, and I do enjoy it. In fact, I've even gone back to school and earned my MBA. But my company knows that I still have to have my own patients, my own one-on-one nursing care. I will never give up that connection with my patients.

When I was finally at peace with what had happened in my life—never forgetting, but moving beyond the "what ifs"—I went on a blind date and met my husband and soul mate. We met for lunch on a Sunday, and the date lasted fourteen hours. Unbeknownst to either of us when the date started, we had both had life-changing experiences that affected our perception of living. I had suffered the loss of my daughter and husband, and he had lived through a car accident that left him with burns over thirty-eight percent of his body. When we were married, the minister referred to us as two half rainbows that had finally joined to make a full rainbow. We have been happily married ever since.

My son Brian—now a young man in his twenties—went through some very difficult times. He has suffered such devastating losses in his young life: not only his father and sister, but also two cousins and five friends. So there has been a lot to work through. His very first counselor—when he was four years old and in play therapy—told me that Brian would go through the stages of grief again when he was an adolescent and as a young man. That certainly was the case. Understandably, he has struggled with depression and with personal relationships. But he is in counseling—and learning to believe that not everyone who comes into his life will leave him. A kind-hearted young man who shows tremendous compassion for others, Brian is in college and hopes to become a pharmacist. He has a remembrance of his sister and dad tattooed on his arm.

A few years after my husband and I married, I heard the tragic news that Dr. Nikaidoh had lost his son in an accident. I was surprised to hear from him several months later, and even more surprised when I realized what he had gone through to find me. He had tried to reach me through Children's, but I had lost touch with my co-workers, and no one had my contact information. He searched the Texas Nurses Association Directory—but he was searching for "Julie Lackey," not my new married name. He even went to the funeral home where we'd held the services for Kimberly and Danny, but they weren't able to help him track me down. Finally, he went through Kimberly's twenty-year-old file one more time and came across a phone number penciled in on the back of a bill. The number belonged to Danny's mother. In fact, Brian was at her house when Dr. Nikaidoh called. I returned his call that night.

He shared with me that it had been painful for him to go back to work at the hospital after his son's death—even though he thought that getting back to work would be helpful. He wanted to know how I had coped with my grief and how I went to work at the very place where I lost Kimberly.

"How do parents get past this heartbreak?" he asked. I certainly don't have the answer for everyone. But I do have the answer for myself. My answer is Kimberly. In her short little life, my daughter brought meaning to so many people's lives, and she inspires me to do the same.

For example, I remember one of the residents who had been at Children's during her time there. Kimberly was absolutely in love with this doctor—as much as a six-year-old can be in love—and you could tell she was special in his eyes, as well. I ran into him several years after Kimberly's death, and I wanted him to know how much he had meant to my daughter.

"You might not remember me," I said. "But I was Kimberly Lackey's mom, and I want you to know what a difference you made in her life."

My words seemed to hang in the air for a second before he spoke, and I wondered if he had possibly forgotten her. But that was certainly not the case. He took a second to compose himself and then said, "I want you to know that I am a better doctor today because of that little girl." Kimberly had that kind of effect on people.

Kimberly's inspiration helps me move forward. In fact, Kimberly's headstone reads "Mommy and Daddy's Angel of Hope, Courage, and Inspiration."

I am also inspired by the difference between Kimberly's death and Danny's: one loving, surrounded by family and friends, the other lonely and sad, surrounded only by a hospital staff who couldn't even take the time to be courteous. This difference inspires me every day to do the right thing, to make the kindest and most respectful connection with those I am treating.

Whether I know my patients on a deeply personal level or not, I know their lives mean *everything* to someone else. I know what their loved ones are going through. When I care for and show respect to those families, I continue my own healing process—and I pass on the legacy of my daughter.

God continued, *"This is the sign of the covenant I am making between me and you and everything living around you and everyone living after you. I'm putting my rainbow in the clouds, a sign of the covenant between me and the Earth. From now on, when I form a cloud over the Earth and the rainbow appears in the cloud, I'll remember my covenant between me and you and everything living, that never again will floodwaters destroy all life. When the rainbow appears in the cloud, I'll see it and remember the eternal covenant between God and everything living, every last living creature on Earth."*

Genesis 9:12–16
The Message

Julie and Kimberly

CHAPTER 4

LINDA SIMPKINS

When I first met AJ Simpkins in 1987, he was a bluish-looking newborn who obviously had problems with oxygen due to inadequate blood flow to his lungs. Even though his mother was still in another hospital due to her C-section delivery, we had no choice but to go ahead with an emergency shunt procedure that day. By that time in my career, I had seen well over one hundred babies with this scenario, and had performed this surgery so many times that I considered it almost mundane. But AJ would teach me differently. That spring morning, I could not have known that my long and difficult journey to try to help this little boy had just begun.

AJ SIMPKINS WAS A big surprise—just a great big surprise all the way around! My husband, Jim, and I were thirty years old when we met, and I already had two little boys. Scott was six, and Ferris was three. Their father had vanished from the family, so I was raising them on my own. When Jim and I married, he adopted the boys right away, and the four of us had a wonderful family together. We were happy, satisfied, and definitely not planning to have any more children at our ages.

In addition, I had significant complications giving birth to my younger son, and my doctor had advised me to avoid any further pregnancies.

But in 1986, eight years after we married, I found myself pregnant.

I was absolutely panicked. Our boys were both doing well in school and were old enough to have some independence. Jim and I both had good jobs, so we were getting on our feet financially. I just could not imagine starting over with an infant! Plus, given my medical history, I had serious health concerns. But after spending the first six months of the pregnancy worrying, I finally came to terms with the fact that, yes, I was actually going to have a baby *at my age.* By the end of the pregnancy, the boys were eager to meet their new sibling, Jim was excited about having his own natural child, and I began to trust that I would be okay physically. We knew from amniocentesis that we were having a boy. We named him Alex James, and decided to call him "AJ."

At the beginning of my labor, everything went well. But when I was almost completely dilated, AJ's heart stopped. Suddenly everyone around me was running, pushing, and yelling. I realized they were getting me ready for an emergency Caesarean—and then I was out.

When I woke up, I could make out Jim and Ferris standing over me, but I didn't see the baby. I was too terrified to think about what had happened to him.

"Is he alive?" I asked.

"Of course," Jim answered.

A flood of relief hit when I saw Scott walking toward me carrying AJ—until I looked at him. Something was not right with this baby.

"Excuse me; do you think the baby's color looks right?" I asked one of the nurses. "Don't you think he looks a little bluish?"

"Oh, no," she said, barely looking at him. "He's doing just fine."

I wasn't convinced. I mentioned his color again to several other nurses, but no one seemed concerned. Later in the day when the new nurses came on shift, I asked them about it too. Again, everyone thought he looked just fine. Eventually, I concluded that this was just how C-section babies looked. I relaxed, and AJ went to the nursery to sleep that night so I could get some rest.

But on the second night of AJ's life, his pediatrician woke me in my room in the early morning hours. AJ had "coded" in the nursery, meaning that he had stopped breathing. I called Jim, and he came to the hospital right away.

"He is breathing now," the doctor told me, "but I certainly wanted you to know what's going on. I didn't hear any signs of a heart murmur, but I've called in another doctor with younger ears—a heart specialist—to listen to him."

As soon as the cardiologist examined AJ, he told us to take him immediately to Children's Medical Center. Because I had delivered by Caesarean and because I was an older mom, my doctors wouldn't release me to go to Children's with AJ. So AJ was taken in an ambulance, and Jim followed behind. Family and friends came to the hospital to stay with me.

At Children's, they ran tests on AJ, and then Jim met with the heart specialist and Dr. Nikaidoh, who explained the test results. Dr. Nikaidoh drew pictures and tried to make everything as clear as possible, but Jim wasn't getting much of it. He was a brand-new daddy and scared to death. Dr. Nikaidoh told Jim that AJ had no chance to live without surgery—but told him honestly he wasn't sure AJ could survive the surgery, either. Jim had my parents, my sister, and my brother-in-law with him, but he didn't want to sign the papers for surgery without me, and I was stuck in another hospital. On the phone, I told him he should definitely go ahead and give permission for the surgery. I was terrified of anyone operating on AJ, but he would die without it, so that's what we had to do.

Dr. Nikaidoh performed AJ's first surgery that very day, and immediately the doctors and nurses saw his coloring change from a dangerous bluish to a much healthier pink. It was only the first hurdle, but AJ had made it.

The following day, I was finally released to go to Children's. I arrived at the medical center in a wheelchair early in the morning.

My oldest son, Scott, and I were allowed to go into the ICU and see him. Although the hospital had sent me a picture of AJ to try to prepare me for what he would look like, I was absolutely devastated by what I saw. Nothing, nothing could really prepare a mother to see all the tubes, the wires, or her baby's shaved little head. I will never forget that sense of shock.

While I stared at AJ, I became aware of a lot of commotion in the room. When I turned around, I saw Scott white as a sheet and three nurses running to his side. One of them was sliding a chair underneath him.

"It's okay, son. Just sit down," she said. "It'll be okay." If those nurses hadn't hopped into action when they did, Scott would have hit the floor, and we could have had another medical emergency on our hands. I doubt it was the first time they had seen a sibling or parent on the verge of fainting. I, too, probably would have fainted from the sight of AJ if I hadn't already been sitting in a wheelchair.

As soon as I knew Scott was all right, Jim and I met with Dr. Nikaidoh in one of the consultation rooms. We were terrified, but as soon as Dr. Nikaidoh came into the room, I felt a tremendous sense of peace come over me. I can't really explain it, but the moment I met him, I trusted him 100 percent. I knew AJ was exactly where he needed to be.

Dr. Nikaidoh explained to us that in a normal heart, oxygen-poor blood returns to one side of the heart and is pumped through the pulmonary artery into the lungs where it picks up oxygen. From there, the blood returns to the other side of the heart to be pumped out to all the body's tissues, bringing fresh oxygen with it. But AJ's heart had not developed normally, and there was no way for the blood to get to the lungs to pick up oxygen. No one can live like that. He explained what he had accomplished in the surgery the previous day and laid out for us the additional surgeries AJ would be facing. He was not very encouraging about AJ's condition. But we felt comforted by his presence and his plan.

I really appreciated all the details Dr. Nikaidoh gave us that day—even if we couldn't remember everything. You come into a situation like that completely helpless, putting your newborn baby into the hands of total strangers. You don't know who these people are, what their skills are, where their hearts are. You only know one thing: You have no choice other than to trust them with your child's life. It is a horrendous experience. But Dr. Nikaidoh told us that day that he would continue to do his best for AJ, helping the whole family through whatever difficult times lay ahead. He said we would be a team working together for AJ. And he told me one more thing that meant so much.

"Linda, I want you to understand that this is in no way your fault. You didn't do anything wrong in your pregnancy or in your life to cause this," he said. "Sometimes these things just happen as a baby develops. We don't know why. It just happens." I desperately needed to hear those very words.

AJ struggled a bit after the surgery, but he made it through all right, and the doctors were satisfied with his progress. When he was about two months old, they said he could be discharged soon. I was ecstatic—until the nurses informed me that I would be responsible for his medications.

"Oh, no. I can't do that," I told them. "I don't know anything about giving medications to a baby this sick. And if I make one mistake, AJ could die."

"But you're a mom. Of course you can learn how to do this," the nurse told me. "We'll help you."

So they worked with me until I felt pretty confident that I could take care of his meds. Then they taught me how to take his blood pressure and other vital signs. Once I was feeling pretty comfortable with all that, they broke the news to me that AJ would be going home with his NG tube, and I had to learn to take care of that, too.

"Oh, no. I'm sorry. I just can't do it," I told them. "I don't know what I'm doing. It's too hard. No."

"NG" stands for nasogastric. It's a tube that goes into the baby's nose, past the throat, and straight down into the stomach. That way, you can feed him by putting food directly into the tube. I had watched the nurses insert the tube lots of times, and of course, it looked easy when they did it. But if done wrong, the tube can end up in the lungs instead of the stomach. From my point of view, they were asking me to do something that could end up killing my son.

But again, the nurses wouldn't take "no" for an answer. They trained me and trained me. Every time I tried it, they were right there telling me I was doing fine, everything was okay. Of course, I never believed them for a minute. But somehow—and only by the grace of God—I was able to learn how to do it.

When the day came to take AJ home, Jim and I and the older boys were thrilled to bring our baby home to finally become part of the family—we really were. In addition to all the excitement, however, I was completely panicked. In fact, the first time I had to put that NG tube in without the nurses standing right next to me, my arm shook uncontrollably. Not only was I terrified of hurting him, but I knew this baby just hated that tube. Even as a newborn—a weak little newborn who had just been through major surgery—AJ hooked his little pinky finger by his nose and pulled that tube right out! I was standing right there and saw the whole thing, and I was sure he was going to die. The nurse calmed me down and explained that it was just the feeding tube. But as a mom, how are you supposed to know what all those tubes are? They all look equally scary and equally important.

The single most worrisome part of having AJ at home was that he could not keep food down in his little tummy. He was on an extra-rich formula because it was so important for him to gain weight, but it all came back up every time I put it in the NG tube. After a few weeks, I called my regular pediatrician, practically in tears. I told him about the NG tube, the formula, the vomiting, and my fears that AJ was never going to grow if he couldn't keep his food down.

He was very calming. "I certainly understand what the doctors are doing at Children's. But let's try something a little different just to see if it works," he said. "Linda, why don't you take that tube out, go to the store, and get yourself a regular old baby bottle with some regular store-bought formula. Let's see what kind of sucking reflex AJ has."

I have never been so happy to give a baby a bottle in my entire life! AJ took to it just beautifully, and the formula stayed down. I relaxed, and I think AJ relaxed. He started gaining weight, and we *all* thoroughly enjoyed having him home. I think that baby bottle was magic.

Just five days after AJ's birth, his little cousin Kyle was born. Since his mother was a single mom, working and going to college, she needed help caring for Kyle. We decided Mom and I would keep him during the day. So we not only had AJ at home finally, but we had his cousin Kyle too. That might sound like *way* too much work. But really, it was wonderful. My mom was always right there if I needed some extra help, and the older boys did everything they could too.

Many things changed for us after AJ's birth, of course. But one thing we had not anticipated was the change in our finances. When I went into labor with AJ, I had a good job as a receptionist at a design company, and Jim had a good job in construction. Our medical insurance, which we had through my job, paid for AJ's first surgery. But when the insurance company realized he would need more and more care, they completely dropped the design company as a client. They would not cover anyone in the whole place just so they wouldn't have to pay for AJ! I was horrified. In addition, it became clear that I would have to quit my job and stay home full time to give AJ the care he needed. We knew that in itself would be difficult financially. But just a few weeks after AJ was born, Jim's company folded.

So by the time we brought AJ home, we had gone from two good jobs with medical insurance to no income and no insurance. We were absolutely dirt poor, just flat broke, with two teenage boys and a very sick baby. Eventually, we had to file for bankruptcy. We simply had no choice.

I worried incessantly about money during that time, most especially as it related to AJ's care. What if he needed help that we couldn't pay for? But Dr. Nikaidoh always calmed my fears. "I don't want you to even think about that," he told me more than once. "We'll take care of AJ first, and then we'll worry about the money later. We are always going to take care of him."

AJ did so well for more than a year, and we all just enjoyed watching this special child grow from an infant into the cutest toddler. But when he was about seventeen months old, he had a heart catheterization that highlighted a serious problem: His left pulmonary artery just did not grow as well as his right, for some unknown reason. At eighteen months old, Dr. Nikaidoh performed another operation to direct more blood flow to the left lung in the hope of enlarging the left pulmonary artery. AJ recovered very quickly, and we were so grateful.

AJ had his next catheterization two years later, and again it showed the left pulmonary artery to be narrower than the right. The doctors were frustrated, and so were we! We knew Dr. Nikaidoh was doing everything he could possibly do to help that artery, but it just never cooperated. And because it was so narrow, it was difficult for AJ's blood to get to his lungs to pick up oxygen. AJ was just past his fourth birthday when Dr. Nikaidoh operated again. This time, he reconstructed the left pulmonary artery. We were so thankful that AJ recovered easily again from the surgery.

In spite of everything, we considered ourselves to be so lucky with AJ. His doctors told us to expect a lag in his development since his oxygen levels stayed so low compared to a normal child. But that never happened. Once he started toddling around at thirteen months old, there was just no stopping him. They had prepared us for cognitive delays, but that never happened either. AJ was absolutely on target. In fact, he was a very bright little boy. The doctors also warned us that he probably wouldn't have the energy to play. That *certainly* never happened! Every single day AJ tried to do whatever Kyle was doing, and his little cousin encouraged him every step of the way. They told us AJ might be light-headed all the time, but we never saw that either.

At one point, I asked one of the cardiologists why they had scared us half to death with such dire predictions.

"Well, the fact is that medically, AJ really shouldn't be able to do any of the things he's doing," he said, shaking his head. "But clearly, someone forgot to give AJ that memo." Thank God for that!

In fact, the quality of AJ's life was just exceptional. Watching him develop, you could almost forget from time to time how broken his little heart was. He was a delightful little boy who just loved being the center of attention—a truly wonderful child.

I tried so hard to let AJ do everything he wanted, to let him be everything he could be. He did not want to be different from other children. So I tried my best to give him the gift of normalcy. The only thing I could not allow him to do was to attend preschool. I just couldn't risk him being hit in the chest in my absence if the kids were playing rough, and I was also afraid of all the germs he could pick up from the other children.

Other than avoiding preschool, we let AJ lead as normal a life as possible. Together, he and his cousin Kyle did everything little boys would do. They played; they ran around; they fought. Looking at those two boys romping around, you would never know anything was wrong with AJ. Sometimes I had to grit my teeth, bite my tongue, and close my eyes in order to allow AJ to be that little boy—to keep myself from constantly reminding him and everyone around him that he was sick and should be careful. But that's the way we wanted it. And more importantly, that's the way *he* wanted it.

In AJ's little mind, he thought that having a broken heart meant he was weak, even though we told him over and over that wasn't the case. He hated thinking of himself as weak. That little boy was so tough—he just would not cry. In fact, if he did get hurt physically, or if someone hurt his feelings and he knew he was going to cry, he would find a place to hide. We told him he should be proud of all he had been through, all he had accomplished. We told him it was a sign of strength. But no matter what we said, he felt very private about it and did not want people to know. He never went around without his shirt, and he hated it when adults asked him to show them his scars.

My older boys just completely embraced this child. They were determined that AJ was going to live life to the fullest and that he *was* going to make it. When AJ was an infant, they were with him all the time, doing everything they possibly could for him. By the time AJ was preschool-aged, my older son, Scott, had a car and always wanted to take AJ for rides.

"Mom, please let us take him with us," he and his brother Ferris would beg.

"Boys, he's not a toy!" I would say.

But off they would go—AJ and the older boys out to get a milkshake or a soda at the drive-through—and I would be left standing there, glued to one spot and just scared to death until they came back.

Later on, when Scott joined the army and left for Korea and my husband Jim was busy all the time working two jobs to try to keep us afloat, it was my middle son, Ferris, who spent as much time with AJ as possible. Ferris was in high school track and field at the time, and AJ and I never missed a meet. After the meet, Ferris would carry AJ around on his shoulders, talking to all his friends. So as far as AJ was concerned, this was "school"—running around outside, laughing with lots of friends, and being the center of attention. No wonder he couldn't wait to enroll!

"Mama, can I go to school now? Can I go? Can I, please?" he would ask me all the time. I would tell him that he had to be five years old to start kindergarten. I'd been able to keep him out of preschool, but I knew that when it came time for kindergarten, I would have to let him be in someone else's care for the day. It scared me badly, but I felt I didn't have a choice.

So that was AJ's life—playing with his cousin every day, track meets with Ferris, birthday parties, games with Scott at Chuck E Cheese™ when he was in town, begging to go to school, and being spoiled by everyone who loved him. Jim and I, our older boys, my parents, in fact, my entire family, everyone just lavished attention on that child, doing anything they could to make him happy. In fact, when AJ and his grandpa bought some carrot seeds for the garden and AJ was devastated that he didn't see carrots within a few days, my dad actually ran to the grocery store, bought some carrots, and stuck them in the ground so AJ could have the pleasure of discovering them the next morning!

Certainly, there were times when we just couldn't avoid the reality of AJ's medical problems. Sometimes he just didn't feel well, when he would be cranky or tire out easily. And there was that very hot summer day when AJ was four years old, running around outside with his two little cousins. All of a sudden, AJ came into the house and leaned up against a wall.

"Mama, I can't breathe," he said, and then he just passed out. It absolutely scared the life out of me. Thankfully, he came to right away, before I could even figure out what to do. When he opened his eyes, he saw me completely panicked. "Mama, I'm okay. Calm down, Mama. I'm okay!"

Not in my book, he wasn't. I called the doctor right away, thinking we'd have to run to the hospital. Instead, the doctor shocked me almost as much as AJ had.

"Are you sure he's never passed out before?" the doctor asked. "You mean this has never, ever happened before?"

"Of course I'm sure. He's looked a little blue from time to time, but that's AJ's normal," I answered.

The doctor said he was surprised that AJ hadn't passed out before due to his low-oxygen saturation, but that it was nothing to worry about in particular. Nothing to worry about? I took a deep breath and decided to keep all the boys in the house for the rest of that afternoon so we could *all* calm down.

Somehow, though, through these occasional "episodes," through all the tests and surgeries, AJ kept his playfulness and great little boy's sense of humor intact. He would bring his toys with him every time he was admitted to "my hospital," as he called it—where everyone on staff led him to believe he was the most important patient in the whole place.

When AJ was about four years old, his brothers bought him some toy guns that shot little foam pellets. He took those to the hospital for his third surgery, when the doctors were planning to reconstruct his left pulmonary artery. All AJ cared about was trying to shoot anyone and everyone. I was mortified, but those guns were his favorite toys, and the staff assured me it was fine. Then one day, Dr. Nikaidoh came into AJ's room to check on him, and AJ shot him right in the face! I was *so* embarrassed.

"AJ, what are you doing?" the doctor asked him. I thought he might reprimand him. In fact, I thought he *should* reprimand him. Instead, Dr. Nikaidoh said, "I'm an un-armed man! You can't shoot an un-armed man!"

"Dr. Kaidoh, there's another gun over here in the window sill," AJ informed him. "You want it?"

The doctor never hesitated. "You bet I do!"

And right there in AJ's room, the surgeon and his patient had quite a shoot-'em-out. It was just what AJ needed, and Dr. "Kaidoh" knew it.

Finally, AJ's fifth birthday arrived. We were all excited and happy, but AJ was absolutely ecstatic. This was the birthday he had been waiting for. The following Monday, he came into our room early in the morning, shouting. "Mama! Mama! Wake up!"

"AJ, what's the matter? What's happened?" I was terrified.

"Nothing's the matter, Mama," he said. "We just have to get up and get ready. Come on!"

"Why? Where are we going? We don't have to be anywhere today."

"We're going to school, Mama," he said. "I'm five now. And it's Monday. That's a school day, Mama. Please, let's get ready."

"Oh, sweetie, school only starts in September," I said, relaxing back into the bed. "You have to wait until the fall, until September, AJ. All the children start together in the fall."

"But Mama, September is too far for me," he said.

AJ had another major surgery scheduled, and he knew it. His recent catheterization had shown once again that, in spite of everyone's best efforts, his left pulmonary artery was still narrowed. And AJ was right: September *would* be too far for him, but I didn't know that yet.

One day a couple of weeks before the surgery, AJ seemed really deep in thought as we were on our way to the grocery store. It was around sunset, a peaceful time of day, and he was just staring out the window lost in a daydream. I asked him what he was thinking about.

"Mama," he said, "do you know where I'm going?"

"I'm pretty sure you're going to the grocery store, AJ."

"No. Mama, I'm going to go see Jesus," he informed me. "And I'm going to hug his neck and tell him 'I love you to the sky.'"

I almost wrecked the car. When I finally pulled over and stopped, I turned around and asked AJ to tell me again what he had just said. He repeated it exactly and seemed to have no idea why I was shocked. I looked at him and took a deep breath.

"Well, AJ, . . . are you nervous or afraid at all?" I asked.

"Mama, don't be *silly*," he said. "Why would anyone be afraid to go see Jesus?"

AJ certainly knew he was sick, and he knew he had heart problems. But we had never discussed death with him. Never. The truth is we never expected him to die so young. The doctors had always been honest with us about his situation, but I guess we just chose to believe there would always be one more thing they could do to help him. That's the way it had been so far. But from this conversation, I learned that AJ felt close to death. I was shocked.

Later in the day, when I'd had more time to think, I realized AJ probably had seen Jesus already. After all, he had coded several times during his life, so I figured he had already seen heaven. Each time that had happened, he'd come back to us, of course. So I'm guessing he never really associated seeing Jesus with having to leave us. He never associated Jesus with dying.

AJ's surgery was scheduled for the end of March, just a few weeks after his fifth birthday. This would be the "fix" that we hoped would provide a permanent solution for his circulation. We knew the surgery was serious, of course, but Dr. Nikaidoh reflected the true depth of his concern when he suggested that my oldest son come home from Korea and be here for the operation. I told him Scott was planning to come home right afterward, when AJ was home recovering and Scott could visit with him. But Dr. Nikaidoh was insistent: Scott needed to be home *before* the surgery. So we worked with the Red Cross and were able to get Scott home in time.

The surgery was long, and we were all so nervous. Four times during the operation, a doctor came out to tell us things looked very grave. They were having a terrible time trying to take AJ back off the life-support system they had put him on for the surgery. His own little heart just didn't want to start working again. Finally, thank God, AJ did make it through. But Dr. Nikaidoh told us he had decided to leave AJ's sternum open, just in case they needed to get back to his heart quickly in an emergency. That was a really scary idea, but we were glad he prepared us for what we would see. The skin was closed, but directly underneath the skin, you could see AJ's little heart beating. It stayed that way for a week. Then, AJ seemed to be making pretty good progress, and Dr. Nikaidoh went ahead and closed his sternum. We took that as a wonderful sign. But our happiness was short-lived.

First, AJ developed a fever. Then a catheterization showed that his left pulmonary artery—the one the doctors had tried to open up so many times—was completely blocked, even worse than before. His liver and kidneys began shutting down. Dr. Nikaidoh explained that AJ had developed what was called "right heart failure" after the surgery. After coming through such a rocky operation, AJ's left pulmonary artery became clogged, and the right ventricle was struggling to send enough blood through the right lung.

But how did that happen? What had happened to the little bundle of energy who had entered the hospital just ten days earlier? AJ was failing, and we knew it.

On the twelfth day after his surgery, I ran into one of AJ's doctors on my way to the hospital chapel.

"We're not going to lose him, are we?" I asked. I hated to hear those words come out of my mouth. The doctor replied carefully and honestly that they were doing absolutely everything possible, but that AJ's condition was very grave. In fact, the doctors had told us that AJ was now at great risk for a stroke or brain damage.

I entered the chapel that day wondering how this little boy— this precious child who prided himself on being so active and so smart—could ever cope with a situation like that. I thought of the little boy who ran around like crazy with his brothers and cousins, who wanted so desperately to go to school. I knew *I* could be all right with whatever happened. I could tolerate anything for AJ's sake. But I couldn't imagine how AJ could tolerate his life with a stroke or brain damage.

And so as I sat down to pray, I opened my heart and poured out my true feelings to God once again.

"Lord, AJ has told me that he thinks he'll see you soon, and he *wants* to see you. I want him to be here with me! I don't want to lose him," I said. "But . . . if he can't get better—if he really can't get better—then I will let you have him back."

I hadn't lain down one time since AJ's surgery. I would sleep sitting up, but I wouldn't allow myself to lie down. Finally, on the thirteenth day after AJ's surgery—the day after I opened my heart to "let" God have AJ back—I laid down. While I was resting, AJ passed away.

AJ's funeral was held in a chapel in Irving, Texas, where we lived. The chapel was completely filled with over one hundred people, and we had more than twenty people standing outside. We were so very moved by everyone's presence. AJ had touched many, many people in his short little life.

When we saw Dr. Nikaidoh come in, we made sure the funeral home found a chair for him, even though they had to seat him in the aisle. Without his skill and heart-felt care, we would never have had our precious boy for those five wonderful years. And yet, when Dr. Nikaidoh filed by AJ's casket, he was sobbing.

"I let you down, little man," he said to AJ.

My father was standing next to Dr. Nikaidoh. Dad put his arms around him and said, "No. You did everything you could."

After the busyness of the funeral, the visitors, and the thank you notes, I was in so much pain that I didn't know what to do with myself. I didn't turn to Jim because I was convinced he didn't understand what I was going through. I would go to the cemetery and just wail, but Jim didn't do that. So I assumed he wasn't hurting all that badly, and I was furious with him! In fact, I was sure that no one in the world had ever experienced as much pain as I was in. I did turn to God, all right, but here's what I told Him:

"Who needs You? I don't want to love anyone anymore! It hurts too much. I don't want it!"

So I handled my pain by becoming a wild child.

I had a single friend at the time who loved to go to bars and dance. She was a wonderful, kind-hearted woman who had spent a lot of time visiting and supporting us at the hospital, and when she asked me to go out at night with her, I went. I would sit there nursing my drink, and men would hit on me. My girlfriend—who danced with several different men—called me a "party pooper" because I wouldn't dance. Thank goodness, I can honestly say that I never danced with anyone, and I never had more than one drink each night. But I didn't exactly turn around and go home, either, did I? As long as I was at the bar with that drink in my hand and watching my girlfriend have fun, I didn't have to think about my pain quite as much. And I'm not too proud to admit that this worked for me for a while.

Thankfully, I eventually came to my senses. I was a married woman with teenage children and here I was hanging out in bars and acting as if I were single! I'm just lucky Jim didn't throw me out in the trash bin. I'm so lucky he's such a good man and that he had a much better understanding of what was happening to me than I did.

What I know now is that grief only comes in one size—and that's "extra large." But each of us responds to that grief in our own way. Some of us cry and scream until we think we don't have any tears or energy left. Others watch television until their minds go numb. Some turn to God with their burden. Some of us hang out in bars. Who was I to think that Jim wasn't suffering just because he acted differently than I did? But at the time, my pain and anger were so overwhelming that I just couldn't see anything or think about anything clearly.

One day not too long after AJ's death, Ferris and some friends were out on the lawn wrestling. One of them did something funny, and I heard a sound that I couldn't place at first. Then I recognized it: It was my laughter. I ran inside and locked myself in the bathroom. Had I really laughed? What kind of a hideous, horrible mother could laugh at *anything* when her baby was dead? I would not forgive myself for the "sin" of my own laughter. That's how upside-down my world was. And it stayed that way for quite a while. In fact, that first year after AJ died was by far the worst year of my life. You would think that nothing could really go wrong after you've lost a child. What else could happen? Well, during the same year I lost AJ, I also lost an uncle, a cousin, and my very best friend. And my father was left paralyzed from a stroke. Just when I would think I couldn't feel any worse, I would be knocked down by yet another loss. All the people I loved who died that year were supposed to help me through AJ's loss! But now they were gone too. I don't mean to put their deaths only into the context of my own personal pain: I know their deaths were painful for many other people as well. But to me, it felt like the bottom of my world had fallen out. I felt as if I had no one to lean on, no one for support. It was as if I were in a free-fall through clouds of pain with nowhere to land.

Until one day, when I hit rock bottom.

At the time, I was working at a manufacturing company just down the road and across the bridge from where AJ was buried. Since it only took about ten minutes to get to the cemetery, I would sometimes go on my lunch hour and visit with AJ. On this particular day, on my way to the cemetery, the weight of my pain and loss had become intolerable. It was absolutely more than I could bear. As I approached the bridge, it occurred to me that if my life were to end, I wouldn't be in this pain. I knew God loved me, and I knew that when I died I would go to heaven and see AJ and all my loved ones again. All I had to do was drive off that bridge, and all my pain would be behind me. That's all it would take.

And with that thought, I'll never forget the feeling of my foot hitting the accelerator.

That's when I heard God say, "Stop. Don't do this."

I drew my foot back. I crossed the bridge, pulled over to the side of the road, and opened my heart up to God.

"I can't take this anymore!" I screamed at Him. "I just wanted to end my own life, but I know I have two sons who need me. You promised not to give me more than I can handle—but You did! You gave me too much. I can't bear it!"

And I heard God tell me, "You're not done here yet."

I answered Him back. "Then you have to take this pain away! I can't do this anymore."

When I calmed down a bit, I drove on to the cemetery and had a good cry at AJ's graveside. Back at the office sitting at my desk, my mind was racing. What had just happened to me? Is this what they mean by going crazy? Had I hallucinated?

And yet . . . later that afternoon, in the middle of typing a letter, I felt the pain leave my body. To this day, I will swear that I felt God touch me.

"You are not here alone," He said. "You will not have to do this by yourself."

I said simply, "Thank you."

And since that day, I have known that God was right there with me. I knew I would have more bad days, and I certainly have! But I have never again felt completely alone. When I finally turned to God, He made me understand that I still had a purpose in my life. All He wanted was for me to turn to Him and ask for help. But I had been too angry. The truth is He had been right there with me all along.

As God lifted the full burden of my pain and loss off my heart, I gradually started my own healing process. I slowly allowed laughter back into my life. Jim and I moved forward, putting our finances back together a piece at a time. Our boys got married, and we were blessed with grandchildren. The loss and the pain were always there, of course. But over time, they no longer controlled our lives. We were fully able to enjoy our grandchildren, watching them grow through the infant, toddler, and elementary years without feeling the pain of missing AJ every single time we looked at them. We focused on our pride in the wonderful fathers our older boys had become.

And we were proud of one more thing, too: Both the boys

had become volunteers working with children—Scott through an Army program and Ferris at Children's Medical Center in Dallas. I was surprised at the time that Ferris was volunteering at Children's, but I was proud of his efforts. While it's true that Children's had done so much for us, I had a hard time imagining Ferris going back to that place where we had also experienced so much pain. He said it made him feel good to give back.

About nine years after AJ's death, Ferris told me he thought I should volunteer at Children's too. By that time, he was working as an Emergency Medical Technician—and in fact, he had met his wife in the ICU at Children's. He also volunteered at Camp John Marc, a camp for children with chronic illnesses or disabilities. And at the recent funeral of one of his campers, he had reconnected with Dr. Nikaidoh.

"Mom, it was so good to see him and say hello," he told me. "It makes me realize how many friends we had at Children's. It was almost like family. Don't you miss them?"

Yes, I had to admit that I did miss my friends at Children's. The people there had been a part of our lives for five years. And I probably knew more people than most parents because I had sold Mary Kay™ to try to make some extra money. So I had friends everywhere in the hospital—in housekeeping, the medical departments, the cafeteria, administration, everywhere. And I did miss them.

But still, to go back to the place where we had lost AJ? I just didn't think I could do it. Luckily for me, though, Ferris never stopped pushing me. In 2001, I finally agreed to try it.

I turned in my application and went for my interview—all volunteers had to go through those procedures—and I told AJ's story during the interview. I still wasn't sure how I would feel about being there—and I didn't want to volunteer unless I really thought I was making a difference. But I was willing to see how it went.

After the volunteer training, I started out as a sitter, just "babysitting" children whose parents needed to take a break, go home, take a shower, see to their other children, or whatever else they needed to do. I'll admit that I was nervous from time to time, not sure I could control my emotions as I saw younger parents facing some of the issues Jim and I had faced. But I found that I did like being back at the hospital. In so many ways, it felt like coming home after a very long absence.

One of the first children I sat with was a little three-year-old girl. That baby was just miserable all the time. The only thing that seemed to make her feel better was leaving her room. I would put her in one of the hospital's little red wagons, hitch up her IV pole, make sure we had everything all set—and then as soon as we turned out of that room into the corridor, she stopped fussing. As I walked her up and down those hallways and saw her face light up with happiness, I knew I was doing the right thing. I really *was* making a difference. I felt a sense of peace in my heart that told me, yes, I was exactly where God wanted me to be.

About three weeks after I started volunteering, I was sitting in a rocking chair holding a little heart baby when I saw Dr. Nikaidoh and another doctor walking straight toward me down the corridor. I had not seen him in nine years, since the day of AJ's funeral. A flood of emotions washed over me, but I just kept rocking as he approached.

When he was close enough to hear me, I said, "Dr. Nikaidoh, you might not remember me but—"

He interrupted, pointed his finger directly at me, and said, "AJ's mom."

"You remember us?" I couldn't believe it. He might have had hundreds of patients since he took care of AJ.

He turned to the doctor he was with, a surgical fellow he was mentoring, and began to tell him everything about AJ's case. He remembered the year of AJ's birth, the details of his heart problems, AJ's ages at his various surgeries, and exactly what the doctors had done at each procedure.

By that time, I was dripping tears onto the head of the poor baby I was rocking.

"How do you do that?" I blubbered.

"How do I do what?" Dr. Nikaidoh asked me.

"How do you remember all that?"

He looked right at me with some confusion and said, "Well, AJ was one of my kids. You didn't expect me to ever forget him, did you?"

At that, both the nurse standing nearby and I started bawling outright. I was completely overwhelmed that this man had remembered my precious baby with such loving detail. He really did think of all of his patients as his children. And when he lost a patient, I realized what an emotionally painful loss it was for him too.

That's why it hit me especially hard when Dr. Nikaidoh lost his own son, Dr. Hitoshi Nikaidoh. We had met Hitoshi several times when he had attended Christmas parties or other events at the hospital. He was such a fine young man and had educated himself to follow in his dad's footsteps. Jim and I were on a vacation when we heard about the tragic accident that took his life, and we immediately packed up our things and went right back home. We couldn't even think of enjoying ourselves when someone we cared about so much was suffering so badly. I would never, ever have wanted Dr. Nikaidoh to feel that pain. I had to force myself to remember that God does know what He's doing. There are so many things we will have answers to one day, but not here on earth.

The next time I saw Dr. Nikaidoh at Children's, he spoke openly about his loss. "I thought every time that I lost one of my patients, I was feeling some of the same pain you parents were feeling," he said. "But until my own child was gone, I did not really know." And then he added something that I still don't understand. He said, "When I see you coming back to this hospital, volunteering to help us with these children after everything you've been through in your own life, you are such an inspiration to me." That's the part I don't agree with: I certainly don't feel like an inspiration. It just makes me feel good to be able to help out.

A few years after I began sitting with the children, I was asked to start a pilot program to establish volunteers in the hospital's ICU. The staff explained they were looking for a mature person, someone who would know what the parents of the ICU children were going through, someone who could relate to them, simply *be* with them, and maybe answer questions. I was flattered that they turned to me and promised I would do my best. The program worked out wonderfully, and I still volunteer there today. It's not always easy, and I'll admit that I sometimes find myself back in the midst of painful memories. But, just like with the little girl in the red wagon, I know I am making a difference. This is what I am meant to do.

I *know* what these parents are going through when they come see their little ones in the ICU for the first time. I can help them understand what all the tubes and wires mean, the same tubes that terrified me so badly twenty-five years ago. I know that by explaining what they're seeing from a parent's perspective, explaining how each tube and wire is supporting their baby, I can help remove some of their own fear. I can't make their baby better—I only wish I could! But I can give them the support and love that I know makes a huge difference. Not many people in the world could give them exactly what I can give. And thank goodness for that, because I wouldn't want other parents to have known my pain. But for the opportunity to help these ICU parents, and for the healing it brings to me too, I am truly grateful. I know God has brought me to this exact point in my life for a reason.

I am blessed that I also had another opportunity to give back to Children's while I've continued volunteering. I'm retired now, but for four years, I worked as an employee in project management as the hospital was going through a major expansion. Every single invoice related to that expansion came through me. It was an awesome opportunity and responsibility to make sure it was all done correctly—to make sure the donated funds went where they were supposed to go, so those who had given money could rest assured it was used to everyone's best advantage. I wasn't a doctor, a nurse, or an aide, but I knew I was making a difference with the professional skills I had.

Today, I still volunteer at Children's. I'm still sitting with the children and still helping the ICU parents. Being AJ's mother prepared me to be able to make a difference in these lives, so I feel this is his legacy, too. I'll never stop missing AJ; sometimes that pain still feels so very raw. But God knew exactly what He was doing when He blessed us with such a wonderful child. AJ redefined me in just five short years, teaching me more about life than anyone else in this world. The little boy with the broken heart who gave so much joy to so many during his short life—he is giving still.

> *You caused me to experience many troubles and misfortunes, but You will revive me again. You will bring me up again, even from the depth of the earth.*
>
> *Psalm 71: 20*
> *Holman Christian Standard Bible*

Linda and AJ

CHAPTER 5

KAREN ELLIS

In 1978 when I began doing heart surgeries for children with developmental delays such as Down syndrome, I was ridiculed and criticized because I was "wasting resources on children who did not deserve them." My longtime friend and patient, Phillip William Ellis, was born with Down syndrome two years later. Phillip and his devoted family showed me and many others the true value of life, with or without a developmental delay. With Phillip's nobility and godly nature, he was a shining guide to us all, and it was my honor to have served as his surgeon.

I DIDN'T SEE MUCH OF my son Phillip at his birth. I was twenty-one years old in 1980 and needed a C-section because he was coming feet first. My husband Jim was in the waiting room, so he didn't see him right away, either. I only got one quick glimpse of Phillip as they lifted him from me during the surgery. He was purple. He was purple and quiet.

"What's the matter with my baby?"

No one would answer me. They took Phillip behind the operating table where I couldn't see him while the obstetrician closed me up. The room was quiet.

"What's the matter with my baby?"

The next thing I knew, I woke up in the recovery room. "Everything's just fine. You just relax now." That's all the nurses would say to me. When my obstetrician came in to check on me, I asked him what happened.

"Everything went well, and you're doing fine," he said. "The baby is in the nursery. Now let's give you something to help you relax."

I was in and out of a drugged sleep for hours. And every time I woke up, I asked for Phillip.

"I want my baby. Where's the pediatrician?"

Jim told me they hadn't been able to find her yet. I couldn't understand. We were in Arlington, Texas, about halfway between Dallas and Fort Worth. Where was the pediatrician? How far away could she be?

At about eleven o'clock that night, she arrived at the hospital—five hours after the hospital had started paging her because there was clearly a problem with this baby. She had been at a dinner party and hadn't answered her page. She came to speak to my husband and me after checking on Phillip.

"Your son is a mongoloid," she said to us by way of introduction. "Do you know what that is?"

"No."

"He needs to go to the children's hospital in Fort Worth. He's what we call mongoloid, and there might be something wrong with his heart."

They wouldn't let Jim ride in the ambulance, so he drove alongside in his car.

The next morning, I saw my obstetrician again. "I need the pediatrician to come back here and talk to me," I told him. "Can you please get her back here?" But no one could get the pediatrician back because she had left that morning for vacation. Her associate did come in for a short time but didn't have much information to offer.

My mother arrived from Connecticut that day, and Jim drove her to Fort Worth to see Phillip. In the meantime, I was moved from the maternity floor to women's health. There were no moms and babies in that department. All I could think about was that I would never see my baby. I just knew they would never bring Phillip back to me.

Finally, a cardiologist at the hospital in Fort Worth met with Jim and my mother. I wasn't there to see this exchange first-hand. But I can picture it as clear as day.

My mother was holding Phillip.

"When can we get my wife and the baby back together?" Jim asked the cardiologist. "Karen is desperate to see him."

"If I were you, I'd never get them back together," the doctor said. "Your best bet is to just leave the baby here and forget you ever had him. He'll be nothing but grief and pain to you, and his heart defect will kill him."

Jim started to ball his fist up as if he were going to slug the doctor, which I'm sure is exactly what he and my mother both wanted to do. But my mom wisely put Phillip into Jim's arms at exactly that moment.

"This is my *son*, and he is going home with *me*," Jim said.

"Fine," the doctor said. "Take him. Do what you want."

"He came over here in an ambulance," my mother said. "We need you to discharge him and get him back to Arlington in an ambulance."

"Oh, no," the doctor answered. "We're not sending an ambulance back there. Just take him. Go on."

So my mother and Jim drove back to Arlington with Phillip. The hospital didn't even care that we had no car seat. They treated my son as if he were a throwaway. And since the doctor couldn't have cared less what happened to Phillip, he certainly hadn't wasted his time calling my hospital to let them know the baby was coming back to their nursery.

Jim and my mom walked back into the Arlington hospital carrying Phillip in a blanket.

"My daughter is here in the hospital," my mother told the nurse at the desk. "So we're bringing the baby back to the nursery."

"Oh, no, I'm sorry. This baby is contaminated. He's been in the outside environment. He can't come back to the nursery here," the nurse said.

My husband's heated response left no doubt as to his thought on the matter.

Eventually, after several more exchanges—and I'm guessing none of them very pleasant—the staff realized my family wasn't going anywhere. They re-admitted Phillip into the nursery and put him in a baby bed in the very back of the room away from all the other babies. Jim asked the nurses to bring him to my room, but they said they couldn't do that because he was contaminated. All I cared about right then was seeing my baby. Now.

So Jim wheeled me down to the nursery. Mom, Jim, and I stayed at the window and looked across the room past all the other babies to the one little bed all alone at the back. That was my first real look at Phillip William Ellis—and at that moment, I fell in love. Right that second, that baby became my whole world. Jim and I absolutely loved and adored him.

We knew Phillip had a heart problem, but we didn't know what our next step should be. We turned to the pediatrician's associate for help, but she told us she was too busy to come back to the hospital. We fired her. That left us without any direction at all.

When my obstetrician came in to check on me again, I told him our problem. He recommended a new pediatrician who set an appointment up to see Phillip as soon as we got out of the hospital, and we were thrilled. As it turned out, she was the doctor who took care of Phillip in the nursery the night he was born.

"Oh, yes, I remember this little guy," she said. And with those three words—this little guy—this doctor became the first person to refer to Phillip as if he were a cute, healthy baby. Compared to how poorly we had been treated, those words were beautiful to my ears. But what she told us next was a shock. "He certainly was not a good cooperator that night. But we got him through."

The more she told us, the more we realized the hospital personnel had been lying when they had continually told us things were "fine, fine." The night had actually been one long battle to keep Phillip from turning blue and staying blue—a battle to keep him alive.

Our new pediatrician recommended a cardiologist at Children's Medical Center in Dallas, and we took Phillip there when he was about two weeks old. After looking at the test results from the hospital in Fort Worth and running a few additional tests at his office, he sat down to talk to us.

The cardiologist explained that Phillip had a condition called endocardial cushion defect. That meant he had just one big open space in the center of his heart instead of the normal four separate chambers. In the normal heart, you have two chambers to pump low-oxygen blood to the lungs and two chambers to pump high-oxygen blood to all the tissues of the body. But because Phillip had just one big chamber in the center of his heart, all of his blood was mixed in there together, diluting the oxygen in the blood that went to his tissues.

Phillip's heart condition would require surgery, probably more than once.

He also told us that Phillip had been born with Down syndrome and would have some mental retardation. When we told him the first pediatrician had called him a "mongoloid," the cardiologist shook his head. He explained that was a derogatory and offensive term. She should never have called him that.

Then we told him what the Fort Worth doctor had said about abandoning Phillip to an institution.

The cardiologist thought for a moment and then took a deep breath before saying, "Look, I'm not in any position to tell you what to do with your child. But I will tell you this: Phillip will be one of the best things that ever happened to you and one of the most hurtful. He will bring so much love into your life, but he will also be your biggest challenge. Just know that I'm here for you. You can call me any time at all, even if you just want to talk."

We were so grateful. After such a hellish beginning, we finally had doctors we could rely on.

Looking back now, I'm amazed at how young I was to handle such challenges! Of course, like most twenty-one-year-olds in love, Jim and I thought we were old enough to take on the world. I had been raised in a strong Christian home and had developed a strong faith at a young age. Plus, I was born under the sign of Taurus the bull! So putting all that together—young idealism, deep faith, my innate nature—I can see how God helped me become a "mama bear" overnight, fiercely protective of my son.

A few days after our visit to the cardiologist, our pastor called to check in on us again. This time, I shared with him my frustration of wanting to have Phillip baptized but being directed by the doctor to avoid public places where Phillip's weakened immune system could put him at risk. The pastor responded by offering to baptize Phillip at our home. So with our parents, our siblings, and Phillip's godparents at the house, Phillip was baptized later that week and joined our church community. I was thrilled!

Our very first job with Phillip was to try to put some weight on him, and the doctor warned us it would be difficult. We were told not to let him cry more than a few minutes at a time. So the minute we heard one peep out of this baby, Jim would rush to pick him up. The truth is we would fight over whose turn it was to hold him; we both wanted him in our arms all the time!

Phillip couldn't nurse because he didn't have a sucking reflex. So we put him on a high-calorie formula and fed him from a bottle with a nipple that had a few extra holes punched in it. We also supplemented with breast milk that I pumped. But Phillip never did gain much weight; he was just a skinny guy his whole life.

At the time of Phillip's birth, I had been working as the manager of a clothing store. As the end of my maternity leave approached, I started researching childcare options. I knew I couldn't take my baby to a traditional daycare. So I responded to an ad in the local paper placed by a pediatric nurse who was looking to keep children in her home. I spoke to the woman on the phone and decided that Phillip and I would go meet her. From the moment she first saw us that day, she had a funny look on her face—a look of surprise. The more I explained about Phillip, the more startled she seemed. Had this nurse never seen a baby with Down syndrome? All of a sudden, she jumped up and ran into the other room, screaming for her husband.

"Honey, come here! You have to see this! It's the baby! It's the baby!"

By that time, I was hanging on to Phillip for dear life and gathering my things to leave. I had heard about baby sitters stealing children, and I wasn't staying around to see what this crazy woman was screaming about. But before I made it to the door, she came back into the room with her husband.

"This is the baby! The one I told you about that I worked on a few months ago!" Then she turned to me and said, "I have wondered so often what happened to him. I just can't believe you're here." I walked back to the couch.

I couldn't believe it either. This nurse had been in the hospital the day Phillip was born, working with our new pediatrician to keep him alive. She was a mom herself who kept children in her home, picking up occasional shifts at the hospital to bring in some extra income. She had placed the ad to increase her childcare clientele—but had changed her mind and pulled it two weeks before I saw it. Someone at the newspaper had accidentally left it in.

I have no doubt in my heart that God brought me to this wonderful woman. She cared for Phillip in her home with kindness and love for several years.

Phillip's first few months were relatively peaceful and uneventful, but when he was about five months old, the cardiologist did some more testing and told us Phillip needed surgery. We trusted him implicitly and were confident in following his direction, but that didn't mean we weren't scared to death. Phillip seemed so tiny and fragile to us, weighing in at a whopping ten pounds.

We checked into Children's Medical Center the day before Phillip's surgery, and that's when we met Dr. Nikaidoh. He took his time with us, explaining exactly what he was planning to do. This was not the larger, more corrective surgery we knew Phillip would need down the road, but this procedure would buy us some time. Dr. Nikaidoh was honest with us. He told us he thought Phillip had a good chance of making it through the surgery—but there also was the possibility he would die. Still, we had no choice. Without the surgery, Phillip definitely would die.

Dr. Nikaidoh didn't sugarcoat anything for us, not at that first surgery or any other time. But he was calm and comforting, and that made it easier for us to hear difficult news. I always had a tremendous sense of peace around him, for which I was very grateful.

The goal of Phillip's first surgery, pulmonary artery banding, was to reduce the rush of blood flowing into his lungs, thus easing the work of his heart. Phillip came through the surgery just fine, but he put us through the wringer afterward. They tried and tried to take Phillip off the breathing machine, but the little guy just wouldn't start breathing on his own. We played that back-and-forth game for weeks. And of course, they had to keep him in the ICU that whole time, which was an additional nightmare for me. The place reminded me of a horse barn with babies in their individual curtained "stalls"—and parents only let in for ten to fifteen minutes every few hours. Finally, after four weeks, Phillip started breathing on his own. We were moved to a private room where I could be with him, and then he was discharged.

"Take him home and treat him just like you would any other child," the doctor instructed us. "But when he cries, don't let him go purple."

And that was our life with Phillip in those early years. We kept trying to put weight on him, tried to keep him from turning purple, and treated him as we would any other child—meaning that we loved him and loved him some more. In response, Phillip did great. He was only about six months delayed, and considering Down syndrome and his heart issues, we were thrilled with his progress. He could color with crayons, string beads, play games, and—when he was a bit older—he learned to ride a bike. While I was at work, our wonderful caregiver would work with Phillip, keeping him stimulated and happy. And on the days when I wasn't at the store, I took Phillip to the Early Childhood Intervention program at the Fort Worth State School, where they taught me how to teach him. It was a wonderful program, and it helped both of us so much. Based on what I learned there, we made sure he had plenty to look at, plenty of stimulation, even before he was moving around much. Maybe that was one of the reasons Phillip was just the happiest little guy you've ever seen. He was curious, cheerful, always smiling. Of course, once he was up and walking, there was no stopping him! He absolutely loved being outside with the other neighborhood children any time he had the chance.

Things were really going well until just before Phillip's third birthday. I started to not feel well—and I panicked. I'd had cervical cancer in college, and I was terrified that it had come back. How could I cope with cancer and care for Phillip at the same time? What if something happened to me? How could Jim care for Phillip by himself?

By the time I got to the doctor, I was just a big ball of anxiety. But when he called with the test results, I was not prepared for what he had to say.

"Mrs. Ellis, I have good news and more good news," he began. "You do not have cervical cancer. You are pregnant."

I immediately started crying. No, I could not be pregnant. This was terrible news. I could not take care of another child with as many needs as Phillip's, and I found it almost impossible to imagine myself giving birth to a healthy baby. I was just scared to death every day until I had an amniocentesis and heard the results I had prayed for: I was pregnant with a perfectly healthy baby boy. Our son Andrew was born later that year—healthy, beautiful, and ours. It was still a lot to handle, an infant and an older child with so many needs. But this was our family, and we loved those boys more than anything in the world.

I had almost made it through Andrew's first year and was just starting to get some of my energy back when Phillip started complaining about a variety of aches and pains.

"It hurts, Mama," he would say, pointing to his legs and arms. And then he stopped walking.

I took him to Children's Medical Center, where the doctor examined him, ran some blood tests, and then told me to make an appointment at the hospital's hematology/oncology clinic.

"What are you saying?" I asked. "I'm not going to wait and wait to find out what's going on. You tell me right now what you're thinking."

"I'm thinking leukemia," he said.

And he was right. Phillip was admitted to the hospital for a few days to begin chemotherapy for leukemia—cancer of the blood cells—and then the majority of his treatment would be administered as an outpatient. I knew children with Down syndrome were at a higher risk for leukemia than the general population—but I honestly thought we had dodged that particular bullet. I guess God had something else in mind.

Just as I was getting Phillip settled in the bed, a man walked into the room wearing a crazy hat with hands sticking up out of each side of the top. He looked like a nut.

I got up and stood between him and Phillip with my arms folded across my chest.

"Who are you?" I asked him.

"I'm the doctor," he answered. "I'm going to be Phillip's oncologist."

"Oh, really? Says who?" No one had told me that a doctor had been assigned to Phillip yet, especially not one who looked like this.

"Well . . . I believe your son was just diagnosed with leukemia. And I'm pretty sure you want him to get better. Am I right?"

"Of course you're right. What do you think?" I said. We stared at each other for a few seconds. "All right. If you're the doctor, you're the doctor. But I've got two rules, and I'm not budging on them. Are you ready?"

He nodded, and those silly hands started waving all over the place.

"Number one: You're here when I need you. Got it? No going on vacation without telling me. No disappearing. I'm not putting up with any crap like that. Number two: I'm not teaching you anything. No one is using my child for any research or training or anything else. He's been through enough. You got that?"

"Yes, I've got it." And he nodded his head again.

Did this guy *have* to nod? I was scared to death, and I did not need those ridiculous hands waving all over the place. Why was I smiling?

As it turned out, Dr. Wavy-Hands-on-His-Head guided us through the twists and turns of leukemia and became a true blessing in our lives. He was not only a stellar oncologist but a fabulous magician as well, as the kids were always excited to see him.

On a cold December day almost a year later, on yet another visit to the hospital, we received the wonderful news that Phillip's cancer was in remission. Santa also was visiting the hospital that day, and it was a blast watching Phillip and Santa together. I was feeling pretty wonderful as I helped Phillip back into his coat in the lobby before heading outside—until he suddenly went limp.

Phillip was completely unconscious in my arms, and no matter what I tried, I could not wake him. So I picked him up with his coat hanging halfway off and ran to the elevators. When the doors opened upstairs, I yelled for our nurse and told her what had happened. She immediately grabbed Phillip out of my arms and ran into a treatment room where they went to work on him. I could see his right arm twitching on the bed.

Scans showed that Phillip had suffered a stroke, which had

caused his seizure, and two previous strokes as well. Later re-search would reveal that children with Down syndrome were hypersensitive to the medications used to treat leukemia. Phillip's chemotherapy had caused those strokes.

Phillip was critically ill, still unconscious, so I guess it was understandable that his doctor wanted to put him in the ICU. But I was flat-out not having it.

"Nope. I'm not putting my child in a room where I can't be with him all the time," I told the doctor.

"But Mrs. Ellis, if he has another stroke, it could kill him," he said. "He really needs to be in the ICU."

"I understand what you're saying. I really do. And I appreci-ate it," I said. "But here's what you need to understand: If Phillip dies, we want to be right there with him. You are not going to put my boy in the ICU where he doesn't know the people or understand what's going on around him. And don't you dare tell him he isn't going to make it."

And that was that. Phillip was out cold for almost four weeks. When he started waking up, I was right there to love on him.

As soon as Phillip regained consciousness, two things be-came clear. First, the strokes had caused him to lose most of his speech. What he had left was slurred to the point of being almost incomprehensible. Later on, he made some progress working with a speech therapist, and we made progress in our ability to understand him. But he never completely regained his normal speech. Second, and certainly more important from a health point of view, Phillip couldn't keep any solid food down. He threw up every single thing he tried to eat. The hospital sent in a specialist who ran some tests and then came to discuss the results with us.

"I'm glad to report we found everything to be normal," he said. "Your son's problem is simply behavioral. He just doesn't want to eat."

"What? Oh, I don't think so," I said shaking my head. "He definitely wants to eat. I mean, even now, knowing that he's going to throw up, he's still trying to eat. That's not his problem.

I'm sorry, but you're wrong."

"I am not wrong. You need to face the fact that your son has some behavioral issues. Mrs. Ellis, this child has Down syndrome."

I stared at this doctor with his pronouncement, my guts all in a knot.

"Really? Down syndrome? You're kidding me," I said. I took a deep breath. "Because, gee whiz, doctor, I've known Phillip his whole life, and I just never realized that."

He stared back at me. "Are you being sarcastic with me? Are *you* trying to tell *me* what is and is not wrong with my patient?"

I considered his question for all of about two seconds.

"No, doctor. I'm telling you this: My son was born with Down syndrome. He has never had behavioral problems and has always loved food—and he is no longer your patient. You are fired. Please leave our room. Now."

It's no real wonder that my nickname at the hospital was "dragon lady." But I had to do what I had to do for my child. I didn't particularly enjoy being bossy or yelling at anyone. In fact, in my life before Phillip, I was quite the people-pleaser—kind, conciliatory, always wanting everyone to be happy and to like me. But when Phillip was born, God gave me a new job, and I guess I just developed a new personality to go with it.

Someone had to keep track of all Phillip's medications and appointments and remember which doctor was for what. That was me. Someone had to stay with him every day during each hospitalization to make sure the doctors and nurses had all the information they needed, to run interference when the right hand didn't know what the left hand was doing (and it happened), and to make sure Phillip understood what was going on and why. That was me. Someone had to fight with the insurance companies and then sue the school district when they weren't living up to their responsibilities to provide services for my son—and win. That was me. But most importantly, someone had to always *act* confident and calm around Phillip so that *he* could feel confident and calm. And that was me.

I'm not saying I did it alone. Jim's parents lived close and were a tremendous support. My parents eventually moved to Texas and were a huge support. My friends and church family certainly did what they could. And I had my husband. But every time something new came up with Phillip—a new crisis, a new procedure to understand and schedule, a new medication to work into our regimen—Jim's response was always the same: "Karen will take care of it."

So Karen did take care of it.

It's not that Jim didn't love Phillip with all his heart. He was the breadwinner and the only one in the family who had a steady job since I had quit working to take care of Phillip. It's that he found it nearly impossible to cope with the worry, fear, and disappointment without being able to *fix* things. I had the Lord to help me carry my burdens. Jim didn't talk much about how he was feeling, and he had his talks with God on his own. My guess is that they weren't pleasant conversations. He kept his feelings bottled up inside until they leaked out in anger at the doctors and staff. Sometimes he exploded at the hospital, and sometimes he just walked out. In his anger and frustration, he even told me once that he didn't believe Philip had leukemia.

"Come on, Karen, he doesn't have cancer," he said. "They just want to run tests on him. The doctors just want to see how kids with Down syndrome react to these medications."

I knew Jim said things like that out of fear because he was in so much pain *for* Philip. He went to work knowing he could count on me to take care of everything, and he came back to the hospital after work to be with Phillip. I understood why he did what he did. But it meant that I was always "on" as Phillip's defender, always had my claws at the ready against any and all intruders just like any mama bear. And with God's help, I mostly did all right—because I had to.

But when I felt myself about to split open with pain, and if Phillip were asleep or had a familiar nurse watching him, I would head to the stairwell, to the area near the double doors. In that place, and *only* in that place, I gave myself permission to stop pretending. Without the pressure to be strong holding me together, I would just fly apart—crying, screaming, cursing God and anyone else I could find, and then crying some more. Finally, I would take a few deep breaths, blow my nose, wipe my face, blow my nose once more, and go back to Phillip. Back to my precious Phillip who did not ask for his life to be framed by a never-ending series of medical crises, who was so polite and cooperative with the doctors and nurses, and who always gave me the same reminder when we prayed together: "I'm okay, Mom. I'm okay."

After I fired the doctor who insisted that Phillip just didn't want to eat, a new doctor ran tests that were more appropriate and discovered that Phillip had developed both an esophageal stricture caused by the herpes virus and a fungal infection caused by the antibiotics he was taking for a heart infection.

Medication eventually took care of the fungal infection, but the stricture just never gave up. Doctors put Phillip under a general anesthetic and dilated his esophagus, hoping that would keep it open. But after we'd been home for a while, Phillip started choking on his food, and we had to come back for another dilation. We hoped it would stay open after that procedure, but it didn't. Eventually, we all realized—the doctors, Jim and I, and Phillip—that keeping Phillip's esophagus open was going to require one dilation after the other, each one in the hospital under a full general anesthetic. For a while, we went for the procedure weekly. Then every two weeks, every three weeks, monthly, and then every six or eight weeks. When Phillip was older, he could tell when he needed another dilation, and we'd just go in as he needed it.

That stricture plagued Phillip for the rest of his life. But he never let that, or anything else, get him down. Phillip was an absolute miracle to me—the way he just kept going, kept pushing on with his life in spite of everything. I have never, ever known anyone as consistently happy and kind and as unfazed by life's hurdles and barriers as Phillip Ellis. When I told him it was time for yet another hospitalization, he would fuss, but he packed his bag. When they told him to stay still so they could poke him for the millionth time, he stayed still. And after enduring yet another bone marrow test or spinal tap, he would turn to the doctor as we were leaving and say, "thank you."

Phillip saw the cardiologist, hematologist/oncologist, neurologist, otolaryngologist, and gastroenterologist. And for several years, he also saw the physical therapist, occupational therapist, and speech therapist. (In fact, the joke around Children's was that the only doctor Phillip didn't see was the gynecologist.) But no matter what, he just didn't complain. He knew these people were there to help him, so he enjoyed their friendship.

However, as he got older, if a doctor didn't speak to him directly, didn't make eye contact with him or treat him respectfully, he would tell me he wanted a different doctor—and we would get him one. In fact, once when Phillip was a teenager, he was so frustrated with a particular doctor that he tried to walk out in the middle of an appointment. I apologized to the doctor and went after Phillip. Yes, I told him, I agreed that the doctor had been rude, ignoring Phillip and speaking directly to me as if Phillip weren't even in the room.

"But still, let's just finish the appointment," I said. "Let's see if this doctor can help you."

But Phillip shook his head and said, "Not my doctor." I followed him out the door.

That's how it was with Phillip. If he felt a connection with someone—someone who was open, comfortable, and fully present with him—that person was Phillip's friend forever. But if an individual wrote Phillip off as "Down syndrome" and wouldn't communicate with him directly, that person rarely got a second chance.

Consequently, thanks in part to Phillip's sensitivity and system of "vetting" people, we ended up with a long-term team of very special doctors—all of whom opened their hearts to Phillip, encouraged us to contact them any time of the day or night, and gave us their home and cell numbers. I think I only intruded on them at night once or twice in all our years together, but just knowing they were available to us gave me a great sense of security. I certainly had friends at the hospital whose children's doctors were not so open and available. In fact, they were shocked that we had our doctors' cell phone numbers. I would just smile and explain, "It's Phillip."

In addition to our wonderful team of doctors, so many people in our lives loved this boy. We had a neighborhood full of kids who played with Phillip from the time they were all little, and all of us parents practically raised each other's kids. We had a church family who embraced Phillip whole-heartedly and whom Phillip loved without reservation. He had friends at every school he attended. And most importantly, Phillip had Andrew.

From the day Andrew was born, Phillip absolutely adored that baby. He couldn't wait for him to be old enough to play. In fact, when poor Andrew was about six months old and not yet crawling, Phillip would grab him under the arms, set him on his feet, and say, "Walk, baby. Walk." I always thought Andrew started walking at a young age just in self-defense!

In some ways, the boys were brothers just like any other pair on the planet. They fought, they played, they fought some more. They built forts, they played ball, and they wrestled and screamed. And at the end of a fight, Phillip would say, "I love you, brother." At which point Andrew would say something like, "Well, if you love me so much, how about don't fight me so hard next time!"

But in other ways, their bond was unique. They had each other's backs with an intensity that most other siblings don't share. If one person said anything the least bit inappropriate to or about Phillip, Andrew would put that person in his place so fast. Andrew was always the peacemaker, always there for Phillip. And after Phillip's strokes left his speech almost incomprehensible, it was always Andrew who could best figure out what his brother was trying to say. Andrew was Phillip's biggest motivator. At medical appointments and in therapy sessions, Philip would listen to his brother over anyone. We counted on Andrew for that.

During all this time, no matter what else was going on, we were also coping with Phillip's heart condition and the surgeries it required. The overall goal of the surgeries was always the same: trying to get more oxygen to Phillip's organs and tissues. God bless Dr. Nikaidoh and how he helped keep Phillip alive for so many years! Before each surgery, Phillip's color would get a little dusky bluish, he would be huffing and puffing when he walked, and he would feel generally pretty weak. In each surgery, Dr. Nikaidoh worked his magic to redirect and rebuild and do whatever he could to get Phillip some more oxygen where he needed it. Afterwards, Phillip would always look and feel so much better. I became a big fan of cardiothoracic surgery!

When Phillip hit middle school in the early 1990s, I started thinking about going back to work. Phillip was relatively stable then, was mainstreamed in school, and his speech had returned to some extent. Every morning, the bus driver would pick him up with a "Good morning, Mr. Independent." And Phillip would give him a smiling "good morning" back. Phillip was so proud of himself for riding that bus alone, and he absolutely loved school. I was so happy for him.

I had been cleaning houses and babysitting to bring in some money when Phillip was younger, and my clients had been very forgiving of my schedule. But eventually, I just couldn't keep up and had to quit. In fact, I didn't work at all for eight years. I had no idea what kind of work I could do or whether I would start a job and immediately have to quit in the face of a new health crisis. Nevertheless, going back to work was on my mind. So when we were at Children's for an annual oncology appointment and the doctor casually asked what I'd been up to, I shared my thoughts about working.

"That's great. We need a receptionist in our department," he said. "Why don't you work here?"

"Oh, no. Absolutely not."

"Why not?"

"Because I hate this place," I said.

"But you'd be great at answering the phones. You know

everything that's going on around here."

"Why in the world would I want to spend any more time in this place than I have to?"

"Because we need you, Karen," he said.

"But . . ."

"Be here Monday morning at seven o'clock. Don't worry about a resume or an application. Just be here."

And that began my career at Children's Medical Center as a receptionist in the Hematology/Oncology Department.

Phillip loved the fact that I had started working at his hospital, as he called it—mostly because he got rid of me for a little while. Like all preteens, Phillip desperately wanted to be just like everyone else, and he also wanted some independence. Since everyone else went to after-school care because their mothers worked, that's exactly what Phillip wanted. A dear friend of mine had just opened a childcare business, so after school each day, Phillip and Andrew would go to her house and play. Phillip could not have been happier. And of course, I was thrilled that he made the transition so easily.

I really enjoyed my new job. The doctor was right—I did know pretty much everything that went on there. Two years later, the department needed an oncology medical secretary, so I moved to that job. After that, I went to work as the office supervisor with a program called ACE, After the Cancer Experience. The ACE staff consisted of a doctor, nurse practitioners, and me. We worked with about 700 patients who were five or more years out from cancer—and that included Phillip. It was a wonderful program that helped these survivors address the lingering medical and social implications of a cancer diagnosis.

Phillip was pretty busy himself in the mid-1990s. He participated in Special Olympics track and field, the softball throw, and bowling, and had a whole wall of medals to show for it. He went to Space Camp in Alabama and became an honorary Space Camp graduate. In fact, an organization called "A Wish with Wings" flew the whole family to Alabama. And at home, Phillip spent a lot of time hanging out with his best buddy, a young man also born with Down syndrome. They would have sleepovers and watch movies until I would finally make them turn the TV off in the middle of the night.

In general, Phillip was interested in all the same things as his peers: hanging out with his buddies, playing video games, pizza parties, watching movies, dancing—and girls. Or, to be precise, one particular girl.

Phillip had met this young lady in fifth grade in his special-education classes. They were boyfriend and girlfriend until she moved away with her family at the end of middle school. After that, they still spoke on the phone every week and mailed presents to each other for Christmas. Years later, they attended each other's high school graduation. Phillip was very much in love and very serious about this girl. He planned to marry her one day and had purchased an engagement ring for her and wedding bands for them both.

Jim was with Phillip when he gave his girlfriend the engagement ring at the airport after her high school graduation. Jim and I just wanted Phillip to be happy, so if they had married, we would have been okay with that too. But the girl's mother was against it, and they could never convince her otherwise. Nevertheless, Phillip was in love and engaged.

Phillip's last heart surgery was in 1998. We had hoped this would be "it"—the big fix we had been waiting for—and at first, everything looked good. But the following year, the new shunt completely clotted off. Dr. Nikaidoh met with us to explain there was nothing more that could be done for Phillip's heart.

Dr. Nikaidoh was clearly distraught, desperately wishing he could give us better news. Phillip patted him on the arm and said, "It's okay. It's okay." That special young man, who did understand what this news meant for him, spent that appointment trying to comfort Dr. Nikaidoh. He never wanted anyone to worry on his behalf. That's just who he was.

Phillip continued with all his regular activities for as long as he could. He participated in Special Olympics, hung out with his friends, and of course he watched his movies. He kept his job at Target for a while, working with a job coach, straightening out the shelves. He even took a few classes at Tarrant County Community College.

Eventually, though, he started weakening and slowing down. But if I showed any concern at all, Phillip would pat me on the hand and say, "It's okay, Mama. I'll be okay. I just need a little rest."

When the time was right, we employed hospice care for Phillip. I'll admit I fought against it tooth and nail—because it made me feel like I was giving up. But they were absolutely wonderful. They always knew exactly how to work with me—and that was no small feat! They knew just what to say and what not to say. I was amazed by their sensitivity. Initially, the hospice nurse came just once a week, making sure Phillip was comfortable, bringing oxygen just in case he wanted it. Once Phillip tried the oxygen and realized how much better he felt with it, he began to use it more and more often. And eventually, as his strength wore out, he started using a wheelchair.

Phillip's hospice nurse introduced him to the firefighters of the Cedar Hill Fire Department through a co-worker of hers. Phillip was invited out to meet the team, see the trucks, and tour the station. It was simply love at first sight. Before the tour ended, Phillip had accepted an invitation to come back for lunch or dinner and watch movies with the guys. Before long, they had "adopted" Phillip and made him an honorary firefighter. We were regulars at the station from that time on—a very special relationship for Phillip.

During those last years of his life, we weren't in the hospital much, usually only going in if Phillip needed a dilation for the esophageal stricture. One day, Phillip announced he was finished with the hospital completely.

"I'm not coming back here to see you again," he told his latest cardiologist. "But you can come to my house and watch a movie with me." He loved this doctor. It's not that he didn't want to see her; it's that Phillip was drawing a line and letting everyone know that he was finished with the poking and the prodding, all the tests and appointments. We gave him the respect he was due and followed those wishes, of course. Phillip Ellis had been so cooperative for his whole life. Now it was time for him to lead the way.

Dr. Nikaidoh did come out to the house to visit Phillip, just as he had made himself available to us throughout Phillip's entire life. Because Dr. Nikaidoh and I were both strong Christians, as was Phillip, it was a great comfort for me to talk with him honestly about what was happening and where Phillip was going after this life. Certainly not all doctors are comfortable addressing the spiritual needs of their patients and families. We were more than blessed to be walking this journey with Dr. Nikaidoh.

During the last year of his life, Phillip was in bed a lot. He still loved his movies, and his friends would come over and watch with him. But that was pretty much his main activity. For family time, we would all get up in the bed with him and watch together. When he wasn't in bed, Phillip was in his wheelchair because walking wore him out so badly.

Phillip tried to prepare all of us for his death, to the very end more concerned about everyone else's feelings than his own. One time in church, when he was still well enough to leave the house, he told me he was going to be an angel.

"You're already an angel, Phillip," I told him. "You're my very own angel right here."

"No Mama, really," he said. "I'm going to be an angel in heaven. I'm going to be okay. I'll come visit."

Or when we'd all be lying in bed together, he'd put his arms around my neck. "I'm going to heaven, Mama, and I'll be fine." Then he would pat my arm and tell me everything would be okay. Everything would be okay. I held onto him for as long as I could.

The night Phillip died, our house was packed with people, just the way he wanted it. Jim and I and Andrew were in the room with him, along with his grandparents, aunts, and his best buddy's mom. Our minister, hospice staff, and neighborhood friends were all at the house. Phillip had orchestrated the gathering, saying that anyone who wanted to come over was welcome.

About five doctors showed up at Phillip's funeral, including Dr. Nikaidoh, of course. Seeing them there, I realized how much they really did care. It wasn't just that Phillip was an interesting case to them, or that I had eventually allowed them to use all of his data in any way that might further their research and help someone else. I had sometimes wondered if maybe that was the reason they seemed to like Phillip so much. But when I saw them at the funeral, I knew for certain that they truly cared for my son. Not Phillip the Down syndrome child with a heart defect and leukemia, but Phillip the loving, kind, generous human being we all strive to be.

The Cedar Hill firefighters were at Phillip's funeral too. In fact, the chief and one other firefighter spoke at the funeral. Their station truck escorted Phillip's casket back to the cemetery after the service.

For the last four years of Phillip's life, I had taken off months and months of medical leave to care for him. But after he died, I found myself working full time for the first time in twenty-five years. Andrew was in college and doing well. Jim was at work. And Phillip was in the care of the One who no longer needed my help.

In the depth of so much grief, I was disoriented for a while, to say the least. I was also often frustrated by the comments of friends and acquaintances who, I have to believe, meant well and thought they were being helpful. But I sometimes wondered.

One person, if not more than one, asked me this: Given the never-ending medical struggles of Phillip's life, the years of my life spent with him in the hospital, the strain on other family relationships, the financial cost—given all that, did I ever wish he had just died at birth?

Did I ever wish my baby had just died at birth?

It is certainly true that our lives were lived within the framework of Phillip's medical needs. Over the course of his life, he had chemotherapy, six heart surgeries, eight heart catheterizations, eight sets of ear tubes, reconstructive hip surgery, and more than 300 dilations for his esophageal stricture. (I made a conscious decision to stop counting at 300.)

But what kind of person would ask such a thing? I've come to believe it's someone who never realized that I loved my child in the exact same way that they loved theirs. It's someone who doesn't see that I suffer the terrible pain of Phillip's loss exactly the same way they would carry the pain of their own child's loss. I believe it's someone who felt I must have loved Phillip less because he was "less" in *their* eyes, someone who never understood that Phillip was created in God's image exactly as he was supposed to be.

The question makes me angry and saddens me terribly. But it's their loss ultimately, because people who would ask such a question had certainly never allowed themselves the pleasure of truly getting to know Phillip Ellis.

I was so grateful to be in the embrace of the hospital when I went back to work. After all, we had been a part of that community for just short of twenty-five years. Everyone had known Phillip and everyone—from the doctors to the administrative staff to the housekeepers—offered their sincere sympathy. They knew the real Phillip here and loved him for the fullness of his whole self. I couldn't walk down the hall without getting a hug. It was a huge relief for me that I didn't have to explain my pain or hide my tears when they would come.

But I was also grateful to have a door to my office. Had I been working in a cubicle then, as I had in my previous positions at the hospital, I would have been "on" all day. But with a door to close, I could let down when I needed to. I could take a deep breath and just be, without always being in the she-lost-her-son spotlight. I was grateful for the freedom to cry in private when I needed to.

A couple of years after Phillip's death, the doctor I was working with at The Center for Cancer and Blood Disorders decided he wanted to start a palliative care program at Children's. He kept talking to me about the program and saying, "This is what we're going to do."

"Oh, no," I told him. "This is what y*ou're* going to do. Not *we*. I am not working only with kids who are dying or chronically ill. At least here at the cancer center a lot of them get better."

"But you're so good at this," he told me more than once. "I've seen you work with the parents at the cancer center. You're so good with them. You have a gift, Karen. I need you to come with me to start a program for palliative care."

"No."

But somehow, he manipulated me until I was a complete believer, completely vested in the idea of starting the program. I realized I could help parents understand that just because something was wrong with a child, it was not the end of the world. In a palliative care program, we could help children have the best life possible, no matter what stage of that journey they were in. I had learned so much being Phillip's mom, so much that I could share with these parents to ease their journey and improve the quality of life for their children. I wanted to put that knowledge to good use.

Once the program was established, I loved it right away. We coordinate care for children with complex, life-limiting conditions and help them enjoy their lives in any way that we can. I'll admit, though, that this job absolutely wears me out some days. I'm sure it would be easier to work at a store selling just about anything—anything that did not involve life and death every single day. But the truth is that I love it here. I love going to work and knowing that good things are happening there, that I am definitely making a difference.

If it hadn't been for Phillip, I never would have been able to give this much. Truthfully, if it hadn't been for Phillip, I never would have known about this work. It just isn't something I would have come to on my own. But having been through Phillip's life and then death, I know how much I have to give to these families. I know what these parents are going through, how frustrated and hopeless they can feel. I know how angry they feel from time to time. And I tell them it's okay to be angry.

Just be sure to use that anger to advocate on behalf of your child! I know what it feels like when the world sums up your child by his disease, without really knowing him as a person at all. I know that hurt first-hand.

More than twenty years ago when I first took that job as a receptionist, I really hated the idea of spending any more time than I had to at Children's. I took the job because I needed to get back to work, and that was the work that fell into my lap. I figured I could tolerate it. But of course, I've come to realize that this is *exactly* where God meant for me to be.

Phillip taught me so much in the nearly twenty-five years of his life. It's now my blessing to put it all to such good use.

Then the King will say, "I'm telling the solemn truth: Whenever you did one of these things to someone overlooked or ignored, that was me — you did it to me."

Matthew 25: 40
The Message

Phillip (front), Jim, Karen and Andrew (left to right)

Chapter 6

SHANNA SHIELDS-THOMAS

On the afternoon of February 2, 2000, my secretary told me that a newborn with hypoplastic left-heart syndrome was on his way to Children's Medical Center. Ethan Shields had been born the previous day with part of his heart missing. The healthy heart has two pumping chambers. The one on the right pumps blood to the lungs, and the one on the left pumps blood to the rest of the body. But children with hypoplastic left-heart syndrome are born with a small, underdeveloped left pumping chamber. Or, like Ethan, they are born with no left pumping chamber at all—and the heart has no way to pump blood out to the body. If left untreated, the infant will live only a few days. So on the second day of his life—at what should have been a time of joy and excitement for his young parents—Ethan Shields was rushed to Children's Medical Center as his parents tumbled into emotional chaos.

My husband and I were so excited about this baby. We wanted him so much. In fact, in a way, Ethan was supposed to save our marriage. Brett and I had been having problems, and I wanted things to be wonderful again—just like they were when I was pregnant with John-John, our first child. So while John-John was still a baby, I decided to get pregnant again. Brett had always wanted a lot of children, so he was thrilled too.

Everything seemed fine, and we could not have been happier. My pregnancy went well. My labor and delivery went well. Ethan started nursing well. Everything felt perfect. In fact, Ethan spent that first night in the room with me, not even in the nursery.

The morning after his birth, they took Ethan to get him ready for his circumcision. Brett went with the baby, and I decided to get cleaned up and ready to go home. But as soon as I got into the shower, a male doctor barged right into my bathroom.

"I just want you to know that we heard a heart murmur," he said. "It's no big deal. We just want to assess Ethan before the circumcision." And he left.

I knew right then that something was very wrong. I couldn't believe a male doctor had just walked right into the bathroom like that with me naked in the shower—without even knocking. That just wasn't right. So as soon as I got out, I called my mother and asked her to come to the hospital to sit with me.

For four hours, my mother and I waited in that hospital room without a single soul coming in to talk to us. Finally, when I couldn't stand it any longer, I went down to the gift shop. On the way there, I passed by the nursery window and saw several people standing around Ethan, all pointing at some x-rays. I went to the nurse's desk to find out what was going on, but no one knew anything. Or no one would tell me.

Frantic, I went back up to the room. And we waited some more.

Finally, the phone rang. It was a woman, and I could tell from the connection that she was calling from a car. She said she was Ethan's cardiologist. She told me my baby had one of the most serious heart defects possible and that the structure of his heart was incompatible with life. Those were her exact words: "incompatible with life." She said we had to get Ethan to Children's Medical Center immediately.

"You have the wrong room," I said. My baby didn't have a cardiologist. And if there *had* been a problem, certainly someone would have come to talk to me about it. "You have the wrong room," I said again.

Then I dropped the phone on the floor and began the crying that would last for days.

"Of course they have the wrong baby," my mother said, trying to comfort and soothe me. "This can't be your baby."

But it *was* my baby. Within hours, Ethan had turned from a healthy, pink, breast-feeding newborn to an ashen baby who could barely breathe. He was taken to Children's Medical Center by ambulance.

Brett and I drove to the hospital and were ushered into the Cardiac Intensive Care Unit consultation room. We met with Dr. Hisashi Nikaidoh, and with hospice representatives and the hospital's transplant team. They explained to us that we had three options.

The first option was simply to allow Ethan to die while providing loving, compassionate care to make him as comfortable as possible. The doctors explained that in the past, this had been a reasonable response to Ethan's condition and a choice that many, many parents had made. They did not recommend it for us. But they said we had every right to choose that for Ethan if we wanted to. Every right.

The second option was a heart transplant. If—a big "if"—an appropriate heart became available in time, a transplant would be the only true way for Ethan to have a structurally normal heart. But if they could not find the right heart in time, we would still face the possibility of losing our baby. And even if Ethan did have a transplant, they explained that his body could reject the heart later on.

The third possibility was a surgery called the Norwood

procedure. With this surgery—plus two additional follow-up surgeries—the doctors could provide a way for Ethan's heart to pump blood to his body. If everything went well in all three operations, Ethan would have a chance to live for ten, twenty, or even thirty years. Dr. Nikaidoh recommended this surgical option. But he also told us honestly that the surgeries were risky and complicated. And there was always the possibility that Ethan wouldn't survive the operations.

Dr. Nikaidoh told us to go home to think about it overnight. But he reminded us that we didn't have much time. He explained that Ethan had seemed fine on the first day of his life because newborns have a small opening between the pulmonary artery, which carries blood to the lungs to be oxygenated, and the aorta, which carries oxygen-rich blood to the rest of the body. But as babies begin to use their lungs, that connection naturally closes during the first few days of life—which is when Ethan began to struggle. By the time Ethan was brought into Children's Medical Center, he had already been put on intravenous medication to keep that pathway open for the time being. That would buy him a couple of days' time. But if we were going to choose the surgery, the longer we waited, the more risky it became.

I hated sitting there talking to these doctors. All I wanted was to hold my baby. I felt overwhelmed with information about things I had never wanted to know. I kept asking repeatedly if we could just take Ethan home. Couldn't we do the surgery when he was six months old? Couldn't we bring him home for a few weeks while we thought things over? Dr. Nikaidoh was very patient with us and very kind. He seemed to have genuine compassion for our situation. But his answer was "no." If we were to choose the surgery, it needed to be done within the first week of life.

So, exhausted, numb, and overwhelmed, Brett and I drove home and left Ethan behind at the hospital.

When we opened the door to our apartment, John-John toddled right over to us. He was 18 months old at the time, and my parents were babysitting him.

"Where's my baby?" John-John asked. That was the very first thing he said when he saw us, and I'll never forget it. I had the same question: *Where was my baby?* My tummy felt so empty. My hands felt so empty.

After we hugged John-John for a bit, Brett and I went out onto our balcony to be alone. We could see all the way from our apartment in the suburbs to downtown Dallas twenty miles away, to the hospital where Ethan was. For a while, we just stood there, feeling Ethan tugging at our hearts. Then I went in and stared at his empty crib. I paced the room and just cried and cried. I think I finally fell asleep on the couch.

We had been so ready for Ethan. We had his clothes in the dresser drawers and diapers in the closet. I even had the diaper wipes already in the warmer. We were so close—so close to being a family with two little boys. It was as if something had been ripped from us when we were right at the finish line.

I had no idea how Brett and I could make the horrible choice ahead of us. I was only twenty years old and felt so young all of a sudden—as if I had never made a major decision in my life. How could we possibly make this choice?

But because there was so little time, we started talking.

First, we discussed the possibility of a heart transplant, and we quickly decided against it. We knew that Ethan would have to be in and out of the hospital for years, and we had another child at home to consider.

Then Brett talked about wanting to go for the Norwood surgery—to do everything possible to give Ethan a chance. And that sounded good at first. But the more we talked, the more we visualized our little newborn going under the knife. What would that be like for him? How much pain would he be in? We just couldn't stand the thought of it.

That left compassionate care. Allowing our child to die an early death, but comfortable, without the pain of surgery. I stared at Ethan's empty crib, and I just wanted him to come home. That's all I wanted. We made our decision. Our baby would be comfortable and in our arms.

The next morning, we drove to the hospital to get Ethan.

It was a terrible drive heading back down the freeway to Dallas, knowing what we were facing. Every mile put us closer to Ethan. But every mile put us farther from the family we thought we would have.

Then all of a sudden, Brett pulled over to the shoulder of the freeway and just started sobbing. He cried so hard. Finally, he said, "I *do* want to put him through the surgeries. I want to give him that chance. I do."

As soon as he said that, I realized that I agreed. Yes, we knew we would be putting Ethan through so much, but we also knew we'd be giving him a fighting chance. And that was a good feeling.

So we finished our drive to the hospital in better spirits, with hope in our hearts. When we got there, we waited with Ethan until Dr. Nikaidoh came in. He shook Brett's hand, greeted me again, and said he was happy to be there for us. The Norwood operation takes a long time, about eight hours, and Dr. Nikaidoh made the decision to wait until the next morning so the team would be fresh.

Brett told me later that he felt good about that visit. "He has good, steady hands," Brett said. "He'll do a good job for Ethan."

The following morning, the whole family was with us at the hospital, except for my parents who were taking care of John-John. We knew it could be touch-and-go. We knew a lot could go wrong. But Ethan made it.

I only saw him for a moment after the operation at the "drive by" window, the segment of hallway between the operating room and the ICU where parents can get a quick glimpse after surgery. My poor baby had so many tubes sticking out of him—tubes were everywhere. The moment I saw him, I felt such a sharp pain of regret. What did we do to him? Why did we put him through this? I felt a sense of panic.

When Brett and I were finally allowed to go into his room and be with him, the nurses told us not to talk. Ethan's heartbeat would increase at the sound of his parents' voices, they said, and that would be stressful for him. In fact, the first forty-eight hours after Ethan's surgery were very shaky and rocky, a very emotional time for us and a physically unstable period for Ethan. More than once, we were told that he might not make it. But each time, he pulled through.

I did not leave the hospital for several days. I waited until Dr. Nikaidoh told me that Ethan's blood pressure was pretty stable and that it was all right to go home. At that point, I realized there was nothing I could really do at the hospital. And as exhausted as I was, I had another child at home who needed me.

Five weeks later, we brought Ethan home for the first time. We qualified for twelve hours of private-duty nursing each night because Ethan needed medication almost every hour. We were so grateful for her help and kindness. Plus, he still had a feeding tube in his nose. Since Ethan didn't have a chance to suck and eat when he was first born, he didn't like having things in his mouth. Consequently, he had the feeding tube to bypass his mouth. But with that tube, he wasn't gaining weight as quickly as he should have. So later on, the doctors surgically inserted a gastrostomy tube that went directly into his stomach, and we fed him through there.

After that first surgery, Ethan really did pretty well. Unfortunately, my husband did not.

Brett had been confused and hurt ever since Ethan's birth. I think he felt like Ethan's diagnosis was somehow a personal attack against him, a personal symbol of failure. So during these first few months of Ethan's life, although I had thought another child would help our marriage, Brett became even more distant from me than he had been. He also started drinking quite a bit. When I discovered he had been hiding alcohol from me, I knew we had a serious problem.

It took every bit of my energy just to take care of Ethan and John-John. And while I recognized that my husband was in pain, I just didn't know what to do for him. Brett and I started fighting, and things got out of control.

It was during this terrible period that I started noticing

Ethan doing something strange. Sometimes when I leaned him forward to burp him, he would curl up into a tight ball for just a few seconds. His eyes would roll up with his eyelids fluttering, and his jaw would clench tight. Then he would relax and sleep for about an hour.

Ethan was having seizures.

I had accepted that my baby had heart problems. But now I had to accept that he had brain problems too? I couldn't understand it.

By this time, Brett and I were hanging on by a thread. And when Ethan developed endocarditis, an infection of the lining of the inside of the heart, it sent Brett over the edge. He started taking out all his emotional pain on everyone around him. He would just scream and scream all the time about how unfair it all was. He reacted to everything and everyone with anger.

"What more bad news could we get about Ethan?" he would yell. "Heart problems. Seizures. And now this. What else can go wrong?" In his pain, Brett became physically violent against John-John and me. The world was crashing in on us.

And then it was time for the second of Ethan's three planned surgeries. Ethan was about six months old then and he had been growing nicely and gaining weight. But the graft material that had been inserted into his heart during his first surgery was inert and couldn't grow with him. Consequently, as he grew, he had less and less oxygen in his blood. We knew this would happen, and we knew that a second surgery would improve the oxygenation of his blood. So it was scheduled.

The doctors prepared us for the fact that this second surgery was also very serious. Once again, the whole family came to the hospital to sit with us. That wait was so difficult, and the surgery seemed to last forever. It was always in our minds that something could go wrong and Ethan could die.

But thankfully, everything went well again this time. Ethan was only in the hospital for five days. John-John spent that time at my parent's house, and I spent the entire five days at the hospital. I never went home. I just felt safer at the hospital than at home with my husband.

On the sixth day after Ethan's second surgery, he was released to come home. I put him in the car, got on the freeway, and called a lawyer on my cell phone to file for divorce. I was apprehensive, and the future was scary. But I realized I could take care of things myself. I was not going to keep living in fear for my children and myself. When I got home, I told Brett my decision, and the boys and I moved in with my parents for a while.

I felt much more at peace in my parents' house, and Ethan continued to do well and grow. We did have a lot of heart catheterizations during those months to dilate Ethan's aorta or other blood vessels, or just to check his progress. But otherwise, no surgeries.

In fact, it turned out to be a wonderful period for us. It was a joy watching Ethan grow from such a sick baby into a mischievous, defiant, strong-minded toddler. And because we were so grateful and happy just to have him, we absolutely spoiled that boy rotten. We never denied him one thing. If he wanted candy, fine. If he wanted an ice pop, fine. He was a noisy, rambunctious, curious little guy with a mind of his own. In fact, if the house got quiet, that meant Ethan was into something. And like most normal toddlers, the word "no" had virtually no meaning for him. He would just look at you and do exactly what he wanted.

We looked at this little boy and laughed at him in wonder— such a problem on the inside, but running around like nobody's business. We figured he *had* to be strong to have weathered all the challenges of his little life. So we just enjoyed the strength of his willfulness and gave in to him all the time.

In the period just before Ethan's third surgery—called the Fontan operation—things were really going well for us. My ex-husband turned out to be a wonderful father to our boys once he and I weren't living together, and I really appreciated that. I had just started seeing a new guy, Corey. I told him right away that I couldn't really get involved because Ethan's surgery was coming up soon, four months past his second birthday. But I deeply appreciated Corey's friendship, and we are still the best of friends today.

We all knew Ethan's third and final operation would be much easier than the others. Dr. Nikaidoh told us that Ethan had a ninety-five percent chance of making it through this surgery. And after the Fontan operation, his heart would be able to pump oxygenated blood to his body, and the blood returning from the body would go through the lungs to be oxygenated—just as it should be.

On June 10, 2002, Ethan was Dr. Nikaidoh's second case scheduled for the day. Since we didn't have to be at the hospital early in the morning, we took our time preparing for the hospital stay. But right before it was time to go, as I was folding one last pile of laundry in my bedroom, I realized the house was oddly quiet. I knew that meant only one thing: Ethan had gotten into something he wasn't supposed to be in. I found him in the bathroom, leaning over the toilet, splashing around with the cardboard inside of a toilet paper roll. The paper itself had been unraveled all over the floor in a big wet mess. That was Ethan—always into something. I scolded him gently to remind him to stay out of the toilet and carried him with me out of the bathroom. It was time to leave, and I couldn't risk him getting into anything else!

The family came to the hospital for the surgery, but they didn't stick around afterward this time. In fact, within an hour after his operation, I was the only one at the hospital. Just Ethan and me. After the surgery, Ethan's toes were pink; his circulation was good. I was happy.

Still, it was a big reality check for me to be there by myself, realizing how alone I was going to be, raising these children. Right then, Corey came down the hall, and I was so happy to have company. I checked in to see that Ethan was doing well, and then Corey and I went across the street to get a meal. I told the nurses where I would be.

Forty-five minutes later, I saw the hospital chaplain in the restaurant. He was walking quickly. Toward me. Ethan had an abnormal heart rhythm, he said. They had already called my family. Brett was on his way to the hospital.

Corey and the chaplain and I ran back across the street, and they took Corey and me into a private room. The ICU doctor told us that if Ethan's heart rhythm became abnormal again, they would have to put him on a machine called the ECMO. I knew the ECMO was the heart/lung bypass machine. And I knew it was the last ditch hope.

"No. You are not going to put Ethan on that machine." That was my immediate reaction. When children are put on the ECMO, they can have a stroke or brain damage. I knew that. Ethan already had a seizure problem. I wasn't going to risk anything worse. But the ICU doctor said they would at least have to move the machine into the room. If they were going to use it, there wouldn't be any time to waste.

Just as my family arrived, Ethan suffered cardiac arrest. Brett and I ran down the hall to his room. For forty-five minutes, they did CPR to try to revive my baby. Dr. Nikaidoh said he would follow our choice about whether or not to put Ethan on the ECMO. Brett left the decision up to me.

I watched them perform CPR on my baby. I weighed the quality of his life versus the quantity.

Then I heard Dr. Nikaidoh say, "Shanna, you have to make the decision. Now."

I looked at Dr. Nikaidoh. "Take that machine out of the room," I said. "We are not putting him on it."

I was so tired for Ethan. I felt like we had done so much to him already. We had done too much to him.

They stopped the CPR and brought us over to Ethan's bedside. The nurses took out all the tubes. I held Ethan close, listening to him take his final breaths. The nurses reminded me that hearing would be his last sense to go. And so I sang. "You Are My Sunshine." "Jesus Loves You." "Somewhere Over the Rainbow."

I held Ethan in my arms until he went cold.

Dr. Nikaidoh spent some time with us as other family

members came in and out of the room. He didn't say much, and neither did we. We were all so deep in our shock and grief. The ICU is usually busy and noisy with lots of equipment and hospital staff. The respirators, monitors, and drainage systems all make noise. But in Ethan's room, all the equipment was gone. It was too quiet—a desolate place in so many ways.

Finally, I left the hospital.

Ethan wasn't supposed to die. He was not supposed to die. Not this time. Not this surgery. Over and over, it played in my head: He was *not* supposed to die. And how was I going to tell John-John that his little brother would never again spend the night in his bed? Never again share his toys, giggles, or bedtime stories? How was I supposed to explain that to a four-year-old? How was I supposed to explain it to myself?

I spent the next four days preparing for Ethan's funeral. I worked feverishly gathering photographs and choosing songs for the computer presentation I wanted to share with everyone. I stayed at my mother's house during that time, surrounded by my immediate and extended family members. Brett wasn't there because he had gone back to his own home to prepare for his family's arrival from out of town. But still, I was never left alone, nor did I want to be alone.

I never slept during those days, not even once. My worst moments were when everyone else was asleep, and the house was quiet. Ethan Shields was all boy—a noisemaker, a mover, his own little action figure. When Ethan was around, nothing was ever quiet. So the silence made the shock of Ethan's death all that much more painful, that much more real.

Dr. Nikaidoh came to Ethan's visitation and to his funeral, and we knew it must have been difficult for him to be there. We knew that Ethan's death had shocked him too and that he cared deeply about Ethan and our family. Dr. Nikaidoh offered us what comfort he could, reminding us that God takes each of us in His time, not ours.

One day during the week of Ethan's death and funeral, my sister took me to a local pet store. She knew that I had always taken comfort in animals and she thought that just being around them might help me, even temporarily. But the trip turned out to be much more than my sister had even hoped for. That's when I found a tiny Persian kitten in a cage, all gray and white. For some reason, she reminded me of the bereavement I was experiencing, so I bought her. Holding her became a huge emotional release for me. I don't know why, but feeling her in my lap as she slept brought me a sense of peace over losing Ethan. It was as if I channeled my deep mourning out of my fingertips and into her soft, pillowed fur. As I heard and felt the quiet hum of her purring, I was finally able to relax enough to sleep again for at least a few minutes at a time.

Sleeping became a huge problem for me after Ethan's death. I was used to him waking me six or seven times a night. Sometimes I would stumble into the kitchen, make a bottle, and stumble back into his bedroom to give it to him. Sometimes I would take him back to bed with me to cuddle and snooze. A few days after the funeral, while I was still at my mother's house, I heard him cry in the middle of the night. So I got up and went into the kitchen. When I realized his cry had been a dream, my knees completely buckled underneath me. I lay on the kitchen floor in front of the refrigerator, just sobbing in the quiet dark of the night. It took all my energy to eventually get up off the floor and back into my bed alone.

I went back to my own home with John-John two weeks later. No one had been in the house since the morning I had left with Ethan for his surgery. The house was musty; I could still feel Ethan in it. His clothes were thrown in a mess in the hallway. His toys were in every nook and cranny. His marbles were left on the couch, as if he had placed them there in that precise arrangement, knowing he was going to come back home and scoop them up, a game left unfinished. I decided that the very first thing I would do was pick up Ethan's toys and donate them to Children's Medical Center. I wanted someone else to be able to use them. So I began to sort them into boxes. And that's when I walked by the bathroom. On the floor was the two-week-old heap of unraveled toilet paper—the mess I hadn't cleaned up before we left for surgery. Looking at the paper, I felt a physical shock go through my system. Our lives had changed so dramatically since the moment that mess had been made. Once again, my knees gave way underneath me.

At that moment, I wasn't sure how I would move forward with my life. I couldn't imagine much of a life beyond the pain I was in. But at Ethan's funeral, I had shared something with Dr. Nikaidoh, a decision I had made that would change the course of my life and become the path that would enable me to work through my grief: I had decided to become a nurse.

Two months after Ethan's death, I entered nursing school full time at Brookhaven Community College in Farmer's Branch, a Dallas suburb. It's usually a two-year nursing program. But since I had never taken any of the nursing prerequisites, in fact never even been to college at all, I knew it would be a four-year program for me. I didn't care. That was fine.

To my family and friends, it might have looked like I was jumping into something without thinking, making an enormous and inappropriate commitment at a time when I was an emotional wreck. A commitment I was in no shape to comprehend, much less complete. I'm sure that's how some of them felt about it. But that just wasn't true.

I had always wanted to be a nurse. In fact, I had entered the Air Force at age 17 because I thought they could put me through nursing school, but that didn't work out. Instead, I had worked in a tech field, which is how I'd met Brett. While I was pregnant with Ethan, I had planned to start nursing school after his birth. But with his heart problems, my plans went out the window. When we were getting ready for Ethan's third surgery, I made my plans once again. This time, I thought I would start school just as soon as he recovered from the surgery. Instead, as it turned out, I threw myself into my classes as a way to work through his loss.

It was so difficult to immerse myself in a world I had never known, while dealing with heavy grief. But that's what I did. I threw my heart and soul into it. Looking back, I don't know how else I would have survived. I wanted so badly to become a nurse. But I didn't realize what a big role nursing school would play in my healing process until school began. It was so good for me to have a schedule, to have a plan to better my future, and to know I was working toward a lifelong dream. It turned out to be one of the best decisions I have ever made.

One of the first things we did in school was work with the charts that assign different point values to various life stressors. Maybe not surprisingly, I had the most stress of anyone in the class. In addition to losing Ethan, I was a single parent to a very confused four-year-old boy. John-John and Ethan had become very close. Watching John-John's confusion was one of the most painful parts of losing Ethan. So with everything put together, my stress index was off the chart.

I worked through it all by studying and learning. Nursing school gave me the opportunity to learn about my stress and my grief. It gave me the opportunity to understand what I was actually going through.

And I embraced it all—anatomy, physiology, microbiology. I learned about the human body and about what I was feeling. I learned that it's okay to talk about it. In cardiology, pharmacology, and microbiology, I did all my papers on topics related to Ethan. I was consumed by learning anything and everything related to him. It made me feel that Ethan was still there. And that's how I began my healing.

During my schooling, John-John was going through his own grieving process, along with trying to adjust to many other changes in his own life. Until I started nursing school, I had always stayed home with him. So not only did he have to adjust to Ethan's death, but he had to get used to being in daycare while I was in school. He was a quiet child in daycare, and his teacher told me he played alone a lot. At night, he slept with "The Brother Bunny," a cuddly brown bunny his grandmother had bought for him the week Ethan died. His father and I, and our whole extended family, did our best to help John-John and to ease the pain of his grieving. But there's no roadmap, no shortcut, no tried-and-true prescription to get through grief whether you're young or old. You just do the best you can.

Just before I began my second year of nursing school, Dr. Nikaidoh lost his son Hitoshi in a terrible accident. Immediately, I thought of the words Dr. Nikaidoh had said to me in comfort the night Ethan passed away: "I will never know what it is truly like to lose a child."

Now he did know, and I wish so badly he never had. I wept for his loss, for I knew the incredible amount of pain he was feeling at that moment. Both my sister and I reached out to him to offer whatever comfort we could. Usually, you don't think about doctors needing help; they're the ones who are busy helping everyone else. But when you lose a child, it doesn't matter who you are—a young, untested woman barely out of her teens or an internationally known doctor, already a grandfather—everyone needs comforting. I left a card and a small flower arrangement on his desk at his office at Children's a couple of weeks after the accident.

Dr. Nikaidoh told me later that my condolences really helped him realize he was not alone. We now live together in a small but strong community—a community where we can share the pain of losing a child.

I saw Dr. Nikaidoh the following year. I was doing one of my clinical rotations at Children's Medical Center, right in the Cardiac ICU. And there was Dr. Nikaidoh. We took a few minutes to talk, to catch up, and he congratulated me for all the progress I had made in my life. I thanked him for his kind words and encouragement and explained that my motivation in nursing was my love for Ethan.

He thought about that for a moment and then said, "It's almost like Ethan himself is in the driver's seat for your recovery."

I graduated from nursing school in December 2005.

What got me through school during that intense period of grieving, and what motivates me still, is one clear desire: I want to be the nurse who took care of Ethan when he arrived at Children's Medical Center. Brett and I spent that afternoon with the doctors who explained the life-and-death decisions we would need to make that very day. But it was so difficult to concentrate in those meetings—because all I wanted was to be with Ethan. I wanted to be the one caring for my baby, touching him, helping him, cradling him. I went to nursing school so that one day, I could be that nurse working in the Cardiac ICU at Children's.

Luckily, I was smart enough to realize that I needed to pace myself. I knew that nurses can easily burn out, and I didn't want that to happen to me. So after graduation, I did not apply for a job at Children's right away. I started off working in the newborn nursery at Lewisville Medical Center and stayed there for eighteen months. I was glad to be working as a nurse, but the newborn nursery was not the right place for me. I did my job very well, but I can't say that I liked it at all. I did not go to nursing school just so I could show perfectly healthy new moms how to breastfeed perfectly healthy newborn babies. That just wasn't me.

As soon as I could transfer, I did. I stayed in the same hospital but moved to the Neonatal ICU, and I loved it immediately. In the NICU, I learned something new every day. And every time I was in there with those sick babies, it brought me closer to Ethan. My heart is just so huge for little sick babies. I feel so much for them, for their families.

Working in the NICU, I was often asked to talk to the parents of the babies with heart conditions. I was always thrilled to do it. They even called me when I was home asleep in the middle of the night to come in to talk to the parents, and I never minded doing that. It was my honor, my mission.

I wish so much that someone had been with me when Ethan was diagnosed. I wish someone had spoken to me directly and with empathy—instead of having a doctor call me from her cell phone in her car to give me such devastating news. Now I can do that for other moms. I can be that person for them. It's definitely not easy, but I've learned that I can do it. I can break the news to the family, be there with them, sympathize, and empathize.

When I have to tell a family about their baby's frightening diagnosis, I do tell them about Ethan so they'll know that I do understand what they're going through. But I do not tell them that Ethan died unless their child dies too. I would never want to take away their hope. If they ask me how he is now, I say, "He's fine now." And I absolutely believe that: He is fine now.

A while later, I made another change that brought me closer to my ultimate goal: I took a position at Children's Medical Center in Dallas in the Post-Anesthesia Care Unit, or recovery room, in the main hospital. I absolutely love it. With each patient, I'm given the opportunity to use my special connection to parents and to children with medical problems. I was even told by one nurse that I would make a great "liaison" because I have a knack for talking to the parents.

The very first month I was at Children's, I was given the opportunity to witness a heart transplant, and I jumped at the chance. When I saw how many people are involved in a heart-transplant case, I was moved to tears. I cried when the diseased heart was removed from the child, and I bawled when I saw the new heart go from a limp, lifeless piece of tissue to become the bright red, beating central life-force for this child.

I also had a chance to work with a child who had heart problems similar to my Ethan's. This child's road had been much harder, though. He had been placed on ECMO to be kept alive at one point in his life, the same machine that I had declined for Ethan. This child was weak, delayed, and kept in his crib. His parents were tearful, and I gave them so many hugs.

After this child left recovery and was taken up to his room, a resident began talking to me about the case and discussing how much ECMO had affected the child. But I stopped her from saying too much. I told her a little of my own story and the decisions I made with Ethan. Then she said to me, "Well, Ethan is in a much better place than that child."

I haven't figured out yet how I feel about that statement and probably never will. Every case is different; every child is different. Ethan might have made it out of ECMO just fine. Or perhaps he wouldn't have. But our decision for Ethan is ours, and I will always stand firm knowing that I made that right call at the right time for my son and my family.

All during my time working at Children's, people would ask me how I could tolerate working there, working at the place where my baby died. But I never looked at it that way! This is the place that gave me Ethan for as long as we did have him. Without the wonderful people at Children's, we wouldn't have had him at all.

John-John and I have both come a long way. He is a teenager now—called "John," not "John-John"—who is busy making friends and finding his niche in school. There have been times when he hasn't wanted to talk about Ethan much because it was his experience that whenever a serious conversation turned to Ethan, someone cried. I do other things to remind him of his brother.

For example, at Christmas, we hang Ethan's stocking on the fireplace mantle. On Ethan's birthday, I take John with me to Ethan's grave. Then we buy a little cake—usually blue with multicolored balloons to remind us of the balloon release we had at Ethan's funeral. We light one candle, sing Ethan the "Happy Birthday" song very softly, and tell him that we love him and miss him so much. Then John blows out the candle. While we eat the cake, we go back to talking about the current goings-on of our lives. I like to imagine that John will continue this tradition on February 1 as he grows up and develops his own independent life—not necessarily buying a cake, but just taking the day to remember his little brother in his own special way.

I also have grown a lot since the time we lost Ethan. I've learned that being at peace with the loss of your child is an ongoing journey, a constant effort. You have to allow yourself the time to grieve. As the years pass, I spend less time grieving. But the moments I do spend in the work of my grief are just as important.

Two years ago, I married a wonderful man and am head-over-heels in love. Jason is an amazing stepfather to John, and he is immensely supportive on Ethan's birthdays and anniversaries. My husband loves listening to stories about his stepson he never got to meet. We live in Colorado now, near John's Uncle Matthew on his father's side of the family. John is really close to him, and I'm so grateful for that relationship. Six years ago, Uncle Matthew named his son in memory of Ethan.

After moving to Colorado, I took a job with a homecare agency—the same agency we had used when Ethan first came home from the hospital. I'm now working as a clinical supervisor managing a staff of more than one hundred nurses, case managers, and other professionals who provide service for more than forty children and adults in their homes. I love the fact that I'm growing into a more mature role in my nursing career. I also love the fact that I speak of Ethan often at work, and my co-workers value his memory as if they had all known him personally. It is because of Ethan that I can do this job now. I know exactly the type of home care my patients—and their families—need.

I will always put my best foot forward to care for those who have been entrusted to me. And I know that when my own time comes to rest, I will take comfort in knowing that I lived my life through this small but powerful legacy of Ethan Shields.

He is called to be the wounded healer, the one who must look after his own wounds but at the same time be prepared to heal the wounds of others.

The Wounded Healer,
Henri J. M. Nouwen,
Image Books, Doubleday, 1979

Ethan and Shanna

CHAPTER 7

MARIE CROWE

In the heat of late August, a newborn boy was transferred to the Children's Medical Center ICU from another hospital in Dallas. The body of this precious infant was massively swollen and distorted; he had been in severe heart failure long before he was born. Our ICU staff worked around the clock to try to keep him alive. With all of his tubes and catheters, we knew he was a sad sight for the parents who kept vigil nearby.

O N AUGUST 22, 1998, I went into labor with my second child, about five weeks before my due date. It had been an easy pregnancy, and the amniocentesis test results were normal, so no one seemed terribly concerned about the early arrival. But just in case, we did have a special-care team, including a neonatologist, in the room.

My husband David and I were ecstatic. We had suffered through infertility for years before our first child, Hannah, was born. Then, without any treatment or medication or planning, we unexpectedly became pregnant with this baby. We could not have been happier.

My labor went slow and hard. Then it became harder and

harder still. I pushed and struggled until I felt like I would never be able to get this baby out. Finally, though, he was in the doctor's hands—and quiet. I waited and waited for the wonderful sound of a newborn's first beautiful cry, but it never came. The team ran with him into the next room to begin working on him.

David and I had expected something so wonderful. Instead, we got hit by a bus.

Jackson Crowe was born with hydrops, a life-threatening condition of severe swelling. This poor little baby was born at eight pounds, but two full pounds of that weight was just water. And just like any part of your body that swells, Jackson's skin was drum tight. Unlike most babies, who are squishy and malleable going through the birth canal, Jackson's body was hard and stiff. That's why my labor had been so difficult.

We found out quickly that hydrops is a description of the baby, but not a diagnosis. We knew our little boy was swollen and in severe distress, but we didn't know why—and neither did the doctors. In the meantime, David and I were in a panic. We felt so helpless. For the first couple of days, no one seemed to have a plan for treating Jackson, a plan for getting him well—and that was what we wanted. We were in a major Dallas hospital with a Neonatal Intensive Care Unit, so we felt like Jackson was getting good care. But was he getting the *best* care? We weren't sure. Should we transfer him to Children's Medical Center, where the top experts in the city could possibly have more to offer? We didn't know.

On the third day of Jackson's life, that decision was taken out of our hands. The doctors told us they believed Jackson's hydrops was caused by a heart problem, and he needed to be treated at Children's. I was just trying to figure out how we would get him there safely, when we learned that the Children's transport team was on their way. From the moment we met the Children's team, we knew we were in good hands. It is quite a procedure just to move a child that sick, but they clearly had done this before. They were competent and methodical, and we were so appreciative. David went in the ambulance with Jackson, and a friend drove me to the hospital separately.

Over the next few days at Children's, we learned that Jackson had been born with a condition called polyvalvular disease, meaning that all four valves of his heart were malformed. The worst problem—and the one most immediately life threatening—was the mitral valve. In a healthy person, oxygenated blood returns to the heart from the lungs, goes through the mitral valve into another part of the heart, and is pumped out to the body's tissues. If the mitral valve is severely malformed and can't close properly, as Jackson's was, the oxygenated blood leaks back and forth through the heart without ever being completely pumped out to the body. The tissues have no way to receive the oxygen they need to support life. None of the four valves of Jackson's little heart had ever worked properly. Consequently, his kidneys were not functioning well; they were not removing the wastewater from his body. Jackson had been born in heart failure, and that was the cause of his hydrops.

Day after day, the ICU team tried to stabilize Jackson and improve his condition to the point that a surgical repair of the mitral valve could be considered. They had Jackson on a procedure called hemodialysis—circulating the blood out of his body, removing the excess fluid, and then re-circulating the blood back in. But if he became strong enough to tolerate surgery, was that even a good idea? We didn't even know what we were waiting and hoping for.

Those were very, very long days for David and me with very little privacy. Most of the ICU parents, parents whose children were as sick as mine, crowded together in the ICU lobby day and night, sharing their stories and traumas—all kinds of people with all kinds of coping skills and family dynamics. The emotional intensity and chaos of those families—most of whom came from out of town and could neither go home at night nor afford a hotel room—was absolutely overwhelming to me.

David and I were so lucky that we lived in Dallas and could go home at night to hug and kiss Hannah and get some sleep. And I was lucky in another respect too. Since I had planned to breastfeed

Jackson and I continued to pump milk for the nurses to give him through one of his tubes, the hospital provided a little lactation room that gave me at least a bit of the privacy and peace I was craving. Of course, whenever the nurses would allow, David and I were in with Jackson, standing by his bed, praying for him, watching with awe and gratitude as the hospital staff took such good, tender care of this fragile little boy we loved so much.

I don't think anyone could have watched those ICU nurses and not been moved by their dedication—not just to the patients, but to the parents too. At such an emotionally chaotic time, it is almost impossible to process the amount of information that comes your way. But the nurses never lost patience, answering question after question with respect and compassion no matter how many times we repeated ourselves. Over and over, they explained the hemodialysis procedure to us and described the vast array of medications helping to keep Jackson alive, the equivalent of "chemical CPR," all of it for the purpose of stabilizing Jackson so he could be strong enough to tolerate surgery. The nurses worked in twelve-hour shifts, not like some places where nurses are in and out all the time and you meet a new nurse every day. These nurses were there for the long haul, for Jackson and for us. And with each day that went by, we valued their support more.

Then, when Jackson was about ten days old, the cardiologist suddenly felt he might be strong enough for surgery, and we met with Dr. Nikaidoh. He told us there was a good chance Jackson would die on the operating table. He also explained that he could not fully know the anatomy of Jackson's heart until he was physically looking at it, so it was certainly possible that he could face unexpected problems. He wanted us to understand that it was completely within our right not to do the surgery, although Jackson's prognosis without surgery was equally bleak. It was not a very hopeful meeting, but we appreciated his honesty because we needed to know the full scope of what we were facing.

David and I did give permission for the surgery. Knowing that it was our only hope, we agreed that we couldn't close the door on a miracle. Dr. Nikaidoh promised us two things—that he would do his absolute best for Jackson and that our baby would have adequate medication for comfort should he live through the surgery.

Jackson was twelve days old when Dr. Nikaidoh performed the surgery—and he did live through it. We knew he was very compromised. We knew he had bad cardiac output and that he had lost his kidney function. But we had been told that if the mitral valve repair held and his heart started functioning better to oxygenate his body, Jackson's kidney function could return. That was the scenario we hoped and prayed for. But that's not what happened.

Although we didn't know it at the time, Jackson's tissues were so thin and damaged that the restructured mitral valve had not held the sutures for any length of time. What we did know, what we could see right in front of us, was that he was not improving.

On the seventeenth day of Jackson's life, David and I both felt that something had changed. That was the day we realized he was not going to get better, even though we had given him every medical chance. It was just not meant to be. Instead of the doctors and nurses keeping Jackson alive to give him a chance for recovery, a recovery that we had believed possible just the previous week, we realized they were now simply working to keep him from death. Jackson had such a slight grasp on this life. David and I both believed it was time to let him go. The doctors, the nurses, the hospital staff who had all taken such good care of our baby—they were all willing to continue providing care, to continue putting those resources into trying to help him. No one told us we had to stop treatment. But it was time.

When we informed the doctors and nurses about our decision, they stopped all the medications, turned off the machines, and removed all the tubes and IV lines. And then, for the first and only time, David and I were able to hold our baby in our arms. It was a quiet room, a dignified space. We held him until his heart slowed down. When it stopped, we knew Jackson Crowe was finally at peace.

David and I left the hospital and went to school to pick up Hannah. We hugged and kissed our only child alive in this world and explained to her the best way we could that her brother had died, that he was in heaven now. We cried that day and every day for weeks. Our hearts were completely broken.

Several weeks after Jackson's death, David and I went back to the hospital—probably one of the most difficult things I have ever done in my life. Somehow, we forced ourselves to drive to the hospital to bring gifts for the staff, going up in the elevator to the floor where Jackson had lived.

Small CD players were brand new then, and we had put one in Jackson's room to play music for him—one of his very few earthly possessions. After his death, we bought the same CD players for the doctors and nurses. It was just the tiniest token of our appreciation for what they had done for us and *how* they had done it. They said they were shocked to see us because so few parents ever come back, which I could certainly understand. Being there was much more difficult emotionally than we had anticipated. It was the site of our worst nightmare.

There were many hugs and many tears that day, and I needed all of them. No words could really say how grateful we were to that staff who had become family to us. We would never forget them, and we hoped that every time they listened to a CD, they would remember Jackson. David and I went home that day glad we had made that trip, no matter how painful.

About four weeks after Jackson's death, I had to do what all new moms do: I had to go for my six-week check-up. There I was, walking into that waiting room filled with proud and tired new moms and newborns still trying to get used to this life. All those wonderfully healthy babies—nursing, wailing, or sleeping with their heads falling over to the side in their carriers. There is no way to describe the amount of pain I was in at that time in my life, and I didn't think it could get any worse. But somehow, it did get worse in that office. Every fiber in my body wanted to run screaming out of that building. But I had a husband and a daughter who needed me, and they needed me to be healthy. So

I sat in the room with the beautiful babies, and I waited for the nurse to call my name.

It's a good thing I did stay for that appointment. That day, my doctor handed me a lifeline by telling me about an organization called MEND: "Mommies Enduring Neonatal Death." I contacted them right away, and David and I became very involved.

To me, the most amazing thing about this group of women was that some of them seemed happy—actually happy. At that point in my life, I could barely remember what "happy" meant, but I recognized it right there on their faces. I knew that every one of these women had lost a child—whether an infant, like me, or through miscarriage or stillbirth. And that meant that at one point in their lives, they had been in just as much pain as I was. But here they were, looking happy. If they had found a way to recapture hope for the future, maybe I could too. By watching their faces, I learned that all hope was not lost.

Initially, I attended every meeting and event for parents who had lost a child, in order to connect with those women. Some of the meetings had breakout sessions for fathers, and David would come too. We also attended memorial events at parks and a Christmas candle-lighting ceremony. At each meeting, each event, I had the opportunity to focus on my grief and only on my grief. For that one period of time, I wasn't expected to be anything else other than a grieving mommy. It was a tremendous release.

One of the issues MEND helped us address was the fact that we didn't have any pictures of Jackson, at least none we could feel comfortable having out in our home. In Jackson's short life, he was never without tubes, wires, or bandages until the very day of his death. Although we did take pictures, and David and I do look at them, they are not pictures to casually share without explanation. It's something so basic, something you take for granted without even thinking—pictures of your child.

MEND told us about a woman who drew portraits of babies with pen and ink, babies who were stillborn—whose parents never saw them with open eyes—or babies who passed away in early infancy like Jackson. I honestly did not think this was for me. She couldn't draw Jackson unless I mailed his pictures, and I couldn't imagine doing that because they were so personal and intimate. But I decided to call her anyway. That one phone conversation put me completely at ease. This was clearly a ministry for this woman. I put Jackson's photos in the mail the next day, and the beautiful drawing we received in return has been displayed in our home ever since.

This artist not only captured his physical features, but she was able to give Jackson something we only wish he could have experienced in this life, and that is peace. In the drawing, he is so comfortable, relaxed, and calm. It gives *us* a sense of serenity to visualize him that way. From a theological perspective, David and I both wish she hadn't drawn little angel wings onto him because we are clear that he was a baby and not an angel. But we decided not to let those wings keep us from enjoying this peaceful version of Jackson.

Jackson passed away in September, and I went back to work in January. I had worked for years in marketing at Johnson and Johnson and had taken seven months maternity leave when Hannah was born. I'm not sure exactly how many months I would have taken with Jackson had things gone according to plan. But after losing him, I certainly needed some time to myself. I went back to work because I felt it would be healthy for me to have some structure in my life again. I thought it would help me heal faster. I was wrong.

My co-workers sincerely tried to be supportive and helpful, but they didn't know what to do. We all felt so awkward. I was so deep in my grief that it was nearly impossible to make it through the workday without crying. It was also impossible to pay attention to all the details of my job. I just didn't know what I was doing there.

As if that weren't enough, I unexpectedly became pregnant and suffered a type of miscarriage—where the placenta kept growing, but the embryo did not—just after I went back to work. In my life before Jackson, that miscarriage would have devastated me. I would have experienced it as the loss of a child—and

I certainly understand and respect mothers who do feel that way. But compared to our loss of Jackson, this miscarriage was merely a blip on the emotional roller coaster we seemed to be living on. It's not that I didn't care. It's just that the miscarriage barely felt real within the setting of my overwhelming pain and grief.

In the end, I quit my job a short time after I started back. I was so lucky to have a husband who could support our family without the help of my income and was willing to take on that responsibility. David and I both agreed that I could best contribute by keeping our family together and just being there for Hannah.

Hannah, who was three years old at the time, had a terrible time with Jackson's death. If I had it to do all over again, I would have made sure she went to the hospital to see her baby brother one time. But we were so immersed in Jackson, overwhelmed with figuring out what to do each day of his life. David and I got up and rushed to the hospital. We were focused on what that particular day would bring for Jackson and grateful that my parents had agreed to move in and stay with Hannah and take her to her first day of nursery school. We would run home for a fast dinner with Hannah. Then back to the hospital.

We just did not have the wisdom to realize that Hannah needed to *see* him to have known for sure that he was real. Three-year-olds deal in the concrete. And her concrete world wasn't making much sense right then. So when Jackson died, Hannah fell apart in exactly the way three-year-olds do it: She insisted on being with me every minute—*every* minute. She followed me through the house, walked with me back and forth to the garage, came into the bathroom with me, and wanted me to hold her all the time. After all, if she couldn't see me, maybe I would disappear too.

I am not a person who thinks there's some type of valor in muddling through problems by yourself when well-trained experts are available help you. We were lucky that we had the resources to access that help. David and I went to grief counseling. We started Hannah with a wonderful play therapist—a specialist who works with the very young—whose work focused on helping children through grief. Both helped us immensely.

The counselors helped David and me understand that we set the tone for Hannah's world in every way at that age. If we were crying, her world was sad. If we were frightened, her world was scary. If we were devastated, her world fell apart. And of course, we were all of those things and more. We had to help Hannah put her world back together. It wasn't a question of pretending that nothing had happened. But we had to let her see that Mommy and Daddy were going to be all right.

Actually, I wasn't convinced at that point that we *were* going to be all right. I wanted to get into bed, pull the covers over my head, and just stay there for months. But nothing was more important to us than helping Hannah put her world back together. So we did our best.

At the beginning of the next summer, about nine months after Jackson's death, Hannah celebrated her fourth birthday. We felt comfortable that her home environment was more normal by then. We still talked about Jackson, of course. But Hannah no longer heard her parents or their relatives or friends telling the story of his death on a daily basis. Her time was taken up with activities, play dates, and wonderful, lazy trips to the pool with me. She was still seeing the play therapist. David and I felt good about her progress.

"Mommy, I have a question for you," Hannah said to me on one of those days in the pool. She and I were lying on rafts and just floating around, as we loved to do.

"Okay, sweetie. What is it?"

"Would you love me if I killed someone?"

"Why, Hannah? Do you think you killed someone?" I asked as I turned toward her.

"Yes," she answered. "Mommy, I killed Jackson."

Those words knocked the wind out of me. I dove into the water and scooped her up in my arms as quickly as I could. "Oh my gosh. No, no, sweetie! No, you didn't kill Jackson." I kissed her face and tucked the wet hair behind her ears. She wrapped her legs around my waist. "Jackson was born a very sick baby.

Remember that? You didn't kill your brother, Hannah. No one killed him. He just died." She put her head on my shoulder.

Who can go into the mind of a little one? Could I really have misunderstood so completely the ways in which this child was suffering?

"Don't you remember I told you she would feel responsible?" Hannah's play therapist asked when I called her. No, I did not remember. I hadn't held much of anything in my mind during those days. "Developmentally, three-year-olds think they're the center of the universe. They believe they have so much power. So if she had any conflicted feelings about him at all, she certainly might believe that she killed him."

Then the therapist explained something to me that I never would have known on my own. She helped me understand that it was much more important for Hannah to get it out—to be able to say everything she was keeping inside—than for me to convince her that she had not killed her brother.

"Hannah needs to get it out," the therapist told me. "She needs to get out every possible theory of how she could have killed him. The best thing you can do for her is to allow her to do that."

I was very grateful for the advice.

Over the course of that summer, Hannah told me several more times that she had killed Jackson. Once she told me she had killed him by getting soap in his eyes. I was confused, since she had never seen him in person and couldn't have put anything in his eyes. Then I remembered that the previous summer, Hannah and I would shower off together after the pool—and she would wash my pregnant belly with soap.

Another time she put it this way: "Mommy, would you still love me if I had killed Jackson?"

If left to my own devices, I would have launched into a big talk about how we don't want to kill anyone because killing is a really bad thing—and on and on and on. I am just grateful to God that I had the play therapist's advice to call upon. I told her exactly what the therapist had suggested.

"Of course, I would still love you, Hannah. I will always love you. There's nothing you could ever do that would change that." And I cradled her in my arms.

Intellectually, Hannah knew she had not killed her brother. She was a very smart little girl. But as the therapist explained, she *felt* that she had. This was horribly distressing to David and me. We were grieving for the loss of our baby, and the pain of that grief was nearly unbearable at times. But at least we did not bear the guilt that Hannah apparently felt on her tiny shoulders. It hurt my heart to think that this precious child felt she bore any responsibility for the very worst thing that had ever happened— and hopefully *would* ever happen—in our family.

Hannah continued to process what had happened in her world, and we continued to support her in any way that we could. She and I spent a lot of time together. I was so happy that I had decided to quit work. Hannah needed large amounts of leisurely time together for these important conversations to develop. Had I still been rushing around trying to get out of the house every morning and coming home to hurriedly throw a quick dinner together every night, I'm not sure exactly when Hannah would have grabbed me to say she had "killed Jackson."

Hannah struggled for quite a while, as we all did. But with time and expert help, she came through just fine. She's a strong, independent teenager now and looks forward to college. Like all of us, she will probably relive the grief of Jackson's loss at various times throughout her life. If that does happen, she knows David and I are right here for her.

Within the first year after Jackson's death, David and I started talking about the possibility of adding one more child to our family—just talking about it. I was already thirty-eight years old, so if we were going to consider another child, we knew we didn't have a lot of time. We had no idea what to do. We felt we needed more time to process our grief and feel secure in our footing before climbing back onto the potential roller coaster of infertility treatments, and I didn't think I had much chance getting pregnant without them. We were so deep in our grief,

nothing made much sense. But I went to see the fertility specialist just to explore our options.

"Marie, if you want to try to have another baby, you just
don't have time to get all your grieving done first. Even if we
started this minute and were successful right away, you'd be
thirty-nine years old when this new baby would be born," he
said. "You just don't have time."

So David and I talked it over. We really did want to open
our hearts and minds to a family of more than one child. On the
other hand, we knew only too well that even with fertility treatments, we might not be able to have another child. We made
our decision, and I called my doctor.

"We're going to go for it," I told him. "Once. One in vitro
attempt. That's it. I don't have the emotional, physical, or financial resources to do it more than once. So we'll go through one
cycle, and if it doesn't work, that's it. We're finished."

Miraculously, I became pregnant with Andy. We were just
thrilled.

Of course, it wasn't exactly a relaxing pregnancy. I was still
going to MEND meetings regularly—this time attending the
support groups specifically for pregnancy after loss. And the
only curse of being involved with a program like that is that you
meet women who have lost children from absolutely every possible cause. Miscarriages and stillbirths and infant deaths from
reasons you never dreamed of—not only bad hearts, but kidneys,
diaphragms, lungs, and pretty much every other body part. And
once you hear about them as a pregnant mom, they just don't
let you go. So between my own tragedy with Jackson and the
stories of all the MEND moms, I pretty much worried my way
through that very high-anxiety pregnancy.

The genetics counselor we consulted at Children's put our
risk of having another child with a significant birth defect as extremely small, only very slightly elevated above the general population. We did a fetal echocardiogram as early in the pregnancy
as reasonable, and it was very reassuring. I really felt that Andy
was going to be okay, and I worked with a team of doctors who

were doing everything possible to ensure that outcome. Best as we could tell, everything looked fine. But still, I worried.

By the end of the pregnancy, it became clear that I might possibly deliver Andy on Jackson's birthday. I did not want to do that. I wanted Jackson's birthday to remain his own. And I wanted Andy to have his own separate birthday. I just wasn't sure I could handle it emotionally otherwise.

When I expressed my concerns to the doctor, he understood. "No problem," he said. "You've got a big healthy baby here. Let's take him a bit early." And so we did. My labor was induced, and I gave birth to Andy just six days before Jackson would have turned two years old.

David and I were absolutely in love with Andy. We had a wonderful, healthy baby, and five-year-old Hannah had the baby brother she had been hoping for. From the outside, we certainly looked like one big happy family.

But no one gets over the loss of a child in a mere two years. And while we were thrilled with our newly completed family, it certainly didn't mean we were finishing grieving for Jackson. That fact of life just seemed so clear to me. But some of our friends and acquaintances didn't understand. Even if they didn't use these exact words, so many expressed this attitude: "Hey— you lost one, you gained one! You're even! Move on!" I think they wanted us to be "over" Jackson both because they loved us and genuinely wanted us to feel better, and also so *they* could be comfortable around us. I was really glad to have the support of MEND at such a perplexing time.

While I would have been *very* happy never to see the inside of a hospital again, David and I still felt a strong emotional tie to Children's and all they had done for Jackson and us. The day we took those CD players up to the doctors and nurses was just the beginning of what would become a great focus of my time and attention—my passion, really—saying "thank you" to Children's Medical Center of Dallas. I doubted it would ever become easy for me to be in that building. But that didn't matter. What mattered was honoring Jackson by helping those who had helped him.

The first thing David and I did was to make a financial contribution. Although we couldn't begin to repay them for the way they had cared for us, we were blessed to be able to make a sizable contribution, and we have continued our financial support in whatever way we can. We created an endowment in Jackson's name to benefit the hospital's cardiac program and continue to fund that. When the hospital was undergoing renovation, David and I sponsored a wonderful sculpture called "Jack Rabbit" that's been placed on the eleventh floor and dedicated in Jackson's memory. We just feel so strongly that we need to do our part to make sure the hospital will be there for other families when they need that care—just like others had done before our time of need. What if Children's hadn't been there for us?

Each year, the hospital holds a wonderful fundraising event that always includes a speaker who can answer the question, "Why Children's?" A few years after Jackson passed away, they asked me to be that speaker. I really thought they'd made a bad mistake.

"Don't you think they'd be better off with someone who had a success story?" I asked David. "I mean there just aren't that many ways to get around saying that you have a dead baby."

But the hospital said they wanted me to tell our story to illustrate the effort the staff puts in for each family, no matter what the outcome. I still wasn't sure. I just didn't know if I could do it without falling apart. But David assured me that if it got to the point where I could not physically speak, he would step up and finish for me. That gave me a great deal of peace. Then I prayed and prayed, and told God that if He wanted me to do this, He would have to do it through me. And that's exactly what happened.

I was completely truthful in telling our story that day. I didn't mislead anyone or leave out any of the difficult parts. I shared honestly that we are on this journey of grief, and it is long and difficult. But Children's gave us time—the time to fall in love with our child and the time it took to know that everything that should have been done *was* done.

It was nothing short of a minor miracle that I was able to finish that speech. Even David said he was amazed at how well I did. So many people came up to me afterward—some of whom had been supporters of the hospital for years and had attended many fundraising events—to say they had never heard anyone articulate the work of the hospital so well. Dr. Nikaidoh was there and congratulated me, too. I was just so glad I could do it. It was a wonderful way for me to thank the hospital and to honor Jackson. Of course, I give all the credit exactly where it belongs, to God.

Over the years, I have also served on Children's board of trustees and as a member of the Women's Auxiliary. Through the Women's Auxiliary, I've worked on fundraising projects, helped with clerical work, served food—whatever I can do to support the staff and parents. This past Mother's Day, we served a special meal for the mothers on the ICU floor so they could fix a plate and take it back to the room. We know they need to be with their children. But we want them to know they are not forgotten on Mother's Day.

"My family told me I had to come out here," one woman told me that day as I helped her with her plate. "This is the first time I've left the room in three days." They are all such heart-breaking stories. I'm just so grateful for the opportunity to give these parents a tiny bit of respite and encouragement. I have walked in their shoes, and I want them to know they are not alone.

I am also still active in MEND, this time as a resource for parents who are closer to the beginning of their grieving process. Many times, I'll get a phone call that goes like this: "You don't know me, but my name is so-and-so. My piano teacher's sister's son's friend just lost a baby. Someone told me you might be willing to speak to her."

Of course I would be. So many wonderful people walked along with me on my journey through grief. I feel obligated to help those who are suffering now. After all, I am one of the relatively few people who understands this particular type of pain. I can tell a newly grieving mother that she will feel better again, and she knows I'm saying it because it's true. I'm probably very insensitive to other kinds of hurts and losses. But I certainly know this one—and I'm here to put that knowledge to good use.

While my passion and my calling is to help these parents and Children's Medical Center in any way I can, I'll admit that part of my motivation is a bit selfish. The only people who ever knew Jackson are right here in this hospital. None of our family, none of our friends ever had a chance to know our baby. But Dr. Nikaidoh knew him and did everything he possibly could for him. The ICU nurses knew him and did everything *they* could. So when I walk into this building to help out—as difficult as it still can be when I step inside—it's also a place of healing for me. The work I do is Jackson's legacy to the children and parents who will find help and solace here in the future. I keep my son's memory alive by being of service.

You keep track of all my sorrows; You have collected all my tears in your bottle; You have recorded each one in your book.

Psalm 56:8
New Living Translation

Jackson David Crowe

CHAPTER 8

LYNETTE DICK

It was early summer of 1986 when a critically ill boy infant was brought to the Children's ER by ambulance from a nearby city. His young, first-time parents did not recognize that he was slipping into serious heart failure. The father was a young preacher, and the family had just recently relocated to Texas. The stress of the recent move, a new ministry, and a sick infant was painfully visible on the anxious faces of the parents. This infant—so scrawny that his diaper just hung on him—was in need of urgent open-heart surgery. In 1986, no other help was available.

MY HUSBAND AND I always joke that our very first meeting took place in a hotel room. Not the normal place to be introduced to your beloved. But that's how it worked out for us.

I was working as a church secretary in Houston at the time and was attending the annual Methodist church conference there with my pastor. Bobby had come to town for the conference, and it turned out that our pastors were best friends from seminary. We all met in his pastor's hotel room to go to dinner before the first night's worship service. Bobby's pastor made sure we rode together in the same car and sat together at dinner and the service. And the rest, as they say, is history. We were married eleven months later, almost thirty years ago now.

I was twenty-one when we married, and I was ready to get pregnant right away. I grew up the youngest of five children, and my mother had been older and not very active in my life. I wanted to be a young mother to my own children, so my plan was to get started quickly and have several children before I turned twenty-five. But Bobby wasn't so crazy about that idea. We compromised and decided to wait until we'd been married for two years before having children, and I went on birth-control pills.

I got off the pill when we had been married about a year and a half, and we figured our first child would be born after our second anniversary. But when I stopped taking the pill, my periods went crazy. They were sporadic, completely unpredictable. We couldn't figure out what time of the month I would be most fertile because there didn't seem to be any "month."

After a while, my gynecologist referred me to a fertility specialist who put me through test after test. At the end of all the testing, he gave me devastating news: I would never be able to become pregnant. I was a very young woman with a deep desire for children. This doctor's news was deeply disturbing, to say the least.

Bobby and I were living in Pasadena, California at that time, where he was attending Fuller Theological Seminary to become a minister. I was working as a bank secretary and sometimes sat in on classes with him on my time off. On the Monday night after receiving such terrible news from the doctor, I attended a class with Bobby entitled "Miracles, Signs, and Wonders." I was listening to the class but also thinking about my own problems. And right then, I realized it was time to turn my fertility issues over to God. I hadn't had a period in three months and had no idea when I ever would again. But I knew that if God had not intended me to be a mother, it was because he had something else planned for me to do.

"Lord, you know the desires of my heart," I found myself praying. "You know how badly I want to be a mom. But I am letting go of control and putting it in your hands. It has to be up to you." Immediately, I relaxed into a strong sense of peace.

The students usually stayed after class for a time of prayer and ministry, and we stayed that night too. After several prayers, one of the teachers stood up and said, "There's a woman in this room who is having fertility problems." He looked around, and I wondered if he could be talking about me. By the time he made several more statements describing this woman—I realized he definitely *was* talking about me.

Bobby and I looked at each other, and then I walked toward the front of the room. The class leaders laid hands on me, and all the students prayed for me—prayed for my fertility to return.

My period began four days later. I became pregnant that month.

I don't think Bobby and I could have been any happier. I had been blessed with the most wonderful of all miracles, and I just could not wait to meet this child. Nine months can be a *long* time when you're pregnant.

As it turned out though, the baby didn't seem to be in any big hurry—in fact, he was fourteen days late. Even after that, it took forty hours of labor and an emergency Caesarean section before he made his appearance. But what a beautiful baby he was! Eight pounds, two ounces—and absolutely gorgeous. For Bobby and me, it was love at first sight.

We were still living in California when Timothy was born, and our house was filled every day with friends and family who knew about our fertility issues and came to celebrate Timothy's birth with us. He was definitely the star of the show. It was such a wonderful time, and we enjoyed every minute of it.

My only problem in adjusting to motherhood was the fact that Timothy was not a good eater. He had problems nursing from the beginning, so we worked with a lactation consultant to get him on track. After that, I thought the nursing was going better, but he wasn't gaining any weight. I decided to augment with formula to put some weight on him that way, but that wasn't successful either. I was a little frustrated that he wasn't gaining weight, but I wasn't too worried. I had taken him to the pediatrician several times, and everything else seemed fine.

Bobby graduated from the seminary when Timothy was just about two months old. We knew we were moving back to Texas, where Bobby would become a minister in the tiny town of Buffalo. I left California first, flying with Timothy to San Antonio so Bobby's parents could spend some time with their first grandchild. Bobby's sister was a neonatal intensive care nurse there, and we told her about Timothy's eating problems. She agreed that he should have been gaining weight and that something just wasn't quite right. But she wasn't able to pinpoint anything in particular.

Then we spent some time in Houston for the annual church conference, staying with a dear friend of mine who had been a foster mother for quite a few children, including several sick babies.

"Lynette, I just think something isn't right," she would say every time she looked at Timothy. "He's looking really scrawny. Please let me take you to my pediatrician."

I agreed. I told this doctor that Timothy had grown in length but not gained even one full pound since his birth. This pediatrician diagnosed Timothy with "failure to thrive," although that really didn't give us much information.

The following week, Bobby, Timothy, and I moved into the parsonage in Buffalo. That Sunday, Bobby preached his first sermon, such an exciting milestone in our lives. We met so many kind and wonderful people that first Sunday, including the local doctor. He had left a fast-paced career in Dallas, slowing down to set up a small general-practice office in Buffalo. He welcomed us to come by any time.

Two days later, we had our worst night with Timothy. He was up all night fussing and crying, and we couldn't seem to get him comfortable, no matter what we did.

"If this baby isn't calmed down and eating well tomorrow morning, I'm taking him to see the doctor we just met," I told Bobby. "I don't know what else to do. Something isn't right."

The next morning, Timothy was still fussy and not eating.

We were waiting for the doctor when he opened his office that afternoon, and he saw Timothy right away. The doctor—whose Dallas practice had been in cardiology—checked Timothy over and listened to his heart. The look on his face was disturbing.

"Come on, let's walk out to your car," he said, standing up. "Timothy is very sick with a severe heart problem. There's no time to describe to you what I think the problem might be. You need to leave right now and drive to the hospital in Corsicana as fast as you can. Don't stop at home or anywhere else. I'll call them right now and tell them to expect you." Although he didn't tell us until later, he wasn't sure Timothy would reach Corsicana alive.

We arrived at the ER less than an hour later. When they drew Timothy's blood, it was black. Absolutely black. They put Timothy and me in an ambulance with a doctor and sent us up to Children's Medical Center in Dallas.

At that point, I still wasn't overly worried. I knew a little girl in Houston who had survived open-heart surgery and was completely fine. And I also knew that a lot of progress had been made in the medical field. I felt confident the doctors at Children's would be able to help Timothy.

The ambulance was doing about ninety miles an hour when we arrived in Dallas, while Bobby followed behind in our car alone. We pulled into the ER dock at the hospital, and before I could even get out, the doctor had scooped Timothy up and was running into the hospital with him. Just as I got into the building, the ER doors closed in my face. That exact moment was one of the most difficult in my life. My baby was in the hands of strangers on the other side of this door, and I was standing alone.

Timothy was in the ER for about an hour. Then they rushed him upstairs to the Intensive Care Unit, where we were only allowed to see him for a few minutes at a time. He was, indeed, a very sick baby.

The cardiologist explained to us that Timothy had been born with a "unicuspid" aortic valve. In the healthy heart, that valve is made up of three flaps or "cusps" that allow oxygenated blood to be pumped out of the heart—through the main artery and into the body's tissues—without leaking back into the heart. It's a one-way valve that looks like a pie cut into three big pieces. But instead of three separate flaps, Timothy's valve just had one piece of tissue stretched across with a very narrow opening in it.

Timothy's was the worst type of aortic valve narrowing. It really wasn't able to function much as a valve at all. The doctor explained that his little heart had been working extra hard to compensate not only since his birth, but throughout his fetal life as well. In fact, his heart had been working so hard that the muscle had thickened as a result. Thickened heart muscle works poorly, completely different from other muscles in the body. His labored breathing and difficulty in feeding were signs that he had gone into heart failure caused by the defect.

Timothy's only chance for survival was surgery to try to widen that valve, and they scheduled it for the following day.

We spent that night at the Ronald McDonald House and went back to the hospital early the next day to meet Timothy's surgeon, Dr. Nikaidoh. He explained to us that Timothy would be put on the heart/lung bypass machine while the surgical team worked to widen the aortic valve. It was an extremely serious operation with so many potential complications—exacerbated by his already weakened heart—but we knew we had no choice.

From the ICU waiting room, we saw Dr. Nikaidoh, his assistant surgeons, and nurses as they wheeled Timothy's bed out of the ICU on their way to surgery. We stopped them to ask if we could take a moment to pray. Not all doctors would have agreed to that, but Dr. Nikaidoh welcomed our prayer. We prayed over Timothy, and we prayed over all the doctors and nurses who would be working so hard to help him. We were grateful for the opportunity.

The surgery lasted about two hours. Afterward, Dr. Nikaidoh explained that Timothy had made it through all right, but the next forty-eight hours would be a critical period. They brought Timothy back up to the ICU, and we went in to see him as soon as we could. We spent that late afternoon in the waiting room with another family whose little boy had also been in surgery with Dr. Nikaidoh that day. And we saw Timothy every chance we could get.

That night, Dr. Nikaidoh had to do emergency surgery on the other boy. Instead of going back to the Ronald McDonald House with Bobby and his mother, who had come in to support us, I offered to stay at the hospital and pray with the other family while their child was in surgery. They were so appreciative. We went down to the snack bar to find a place to sit with a bit of privacy, since the main cafeteria was closed for the night.

We'd been talking and praying together for a while when a nurse came running in and turned toward us. We all knew by the look on her face that one of the children was in trouble—we just didn't know yet which child. It was as if the scene were happening in slow motion.

"Mrs. Dick, you need to come quickly," she said.

As soon as I got upstairs with the nurse, they told me Timothy had "coded," meaning he had stopped breathing, and they were doing their best to revive him. I asked them to call my husband at the Ronald McDonald House.

While they did that, I called people to get prayer chains started all over the country. That was in the days before cell phones, and since I didn't have a pocketful of change for the pay phone, I had to call everyone collect. Although I knew my child was near death, I didn't ask anyone to pray for God to keep Timothy alive. The prayer that God put on my heart was this: "Jesus, be with him. And let him know his parents love him." Later on when I thought about it, I came to believe that God put that particular prayer on my heart because it was one He could answer with "yes."

Timothy had had a heart attack after his surgery. The fact that his heart had been working extra hard since before his birth to compensate for the narrowing of the aortic valve had caused the heart wall to thicken and weaken. His heart muscle just wasn't able to withstand the stress any longer.

The doctors worked on Timothy for a good forty-five minutes. I think they knew they wouldn't be able to revive him, but they kept working on him until Bobby arrived so they could tell both of us together. Once they pronounced Timothy deceased, they cleaned him up and brought him into the family room so we could hold him for a while. Then we had to say goodbye to our precious boy who had lived for only fourteen weeks.

Dr. Nikaidoh was still in the operating room trying to save the other child's life when Timothy died. Although we didn't have a chance to speak to him before leaving the hospital, we received a phone call from him later in the day and a beautiful, heart-felt card that we have kept to this day. He only knew our Timothy for such a few hours, but his compassion for our family touched us deeply.

Bobby and I went back to the Ronald McDonald House in the early morning hours and crawled into one of the twin beds together while his mother slept in the other. I doubt we got any sleep, but we hung onto each other for dear life.

Timothy passed away on the Friday before Father's Day. That Sunday morning, instead of going to church and celebrating what would have been Bobby's first Father's Day, we set out for Houston, where we had decided to hold Timothy's funeral. On Father's Day, we bought a casket for our son.

When such a young couple loses a child, how can friends and relatives possibly know how to comfort them? Most of those friends are young people, too—many of whom have barely started their own families or are just getting ready to. They cannot know how it feels—and thank God for that! In fact, because the concept of losing a baby raises such terrible fear, many people can't even allow themselves to *imagine* how the loss feels. And I don't blame them for that. It's just so painful for everyone; no one really knows what to say.

I would never want any parent to have to go through what we went through: To be told you could never have children, then to become pregnant, then to have your baby taken away so quickly! It was really more than any human could bear. In fact, I don't believe there *is* a human way to get through it. I was twenty-four years old, so young! Without God's grace—without absolutely knowing one hundred percent that Timothy was with Jesus, exactly where he needed to be—I have no idea how I would have lived through such an unbelievable loss.

Bobby and I made it through the funeral somehow, but once we were back in Buffalo, just the two of us alone in the parsonage without our baby, we struggled terribly. There were tears, of course, lots of tears. But my grief also came out in anger.

I was *so* angry. I just felt furious day and night. I would become irate at the least little thing—screaming, yelling, and saying mean, horrible things. I was in so much pain; I just didn't know what to do. The pain just poured out of me in a rage, day after day.

My anger wasn't directed at God. I knew that Timothy had belonged to God all along, so I wasn't angry that God had taken him back in His own timing. I also knew that Timothy had had such a hard, painful time on this earth, so I was genuinely grateful that he was beyond pain now.

But I was furious at the man in the car ahead of me who took three seconds too long to move through the stop sign. I wanted to curse out the pharmacy clerk because she made a mistake at checkout. Or the weatherman on TV because it was so darn hot. I was even angry with the child who dropped something right in front of my grocery cart and forced me to slow down.

What I know for sure is that I took all my anger out on the only person available to me. I was filled with such a terrible rage, and it spilled out on my poor husband day after day. The man deserves sainthood for what he put up with from me.

Then one day several months after Timothy's death, when I was in the middle of one of my tirades, I suddenly saw with clarity what was happening. And in that epiphany, I just collapsed.

"I am so sorry," I told Bobby through my sobbing. "I have been beating you up through my words over and over again because of this terrible pain I have inside me. But I never stopped to think that you have the very same pain! You buried your son too."

I am just a lucky woman that Bobby understood me and forgave me for that behavior. Poor Bobby had no one for support.

When a couple faces a tragedy like this, everyone seems to rally around the mother, offering support best as they can. But the fathers are just out there on their own. They've been trained their whole lives not to show their painful or sad feelings, to keep it to themselves no matter what. And instead of supporting my husband when he needed it most, the intensity of my own pain absolutely blinded me to his needs.

That was a turning point in our relationship. We had heard that eighty percent of couples who experience a tragedy like ours end up divorced. We knew we had to be in the other twenty percent—we just needed to learn to better support each other through this tragedy, to come together instead of ripping ourselves apart. From that point on, I made sure that my pain manifested itself in less hurtful ways.

While having another child certainly was not on my mind right after Timothy's death, I was frustrated that my periods had become irregular again. I'd had one period the week of Timothy's death and then nothing. But about ten weeks or so after Timothy's death, I discovered the reason for the missing periods: I was pregnant. The pregnancy was not anything we had planned, and it was certainly a shock for both Bobby and me—but we were ecstatic.

My family and friends were not quite so happy. No one said anything directly to me at first. But some months into my pregnancy, one of my very dear friends expressed the concern shared by many others.

"Lynette, I'm just worried that you're trying to replace Timothy by having another baby so soon," she said. "Do you really feel ready for this? We're all praying for a girl, just so you'd never be tempted to 'pretend' this baby was Timothy."

But I assured her, and everyone else, that I knew I could never replace Timothy, nor would I ever want to.

"I know exactly where Timothy is," I told her. "His body is in the ground, and his spirit is in heaven. Timothy was my first miracle. The baby I'm carrying now is my second."

I was genuinely thrilled to be pregnant. But I was also

simultaneously grieving for Timothy and worried about the health of the baby I was carrying. We had been told that defects on the left side of the heart, which Timothy's was, tend to be hereditary. So I kept wondering how long I would be allowed to keep this new baby. When would he be taken from me?

My obstetrician offered to do a sonogram to check the structure of the baby's heart, suggesting that if a problem were discovered I could abort the pregnancy. But since I would never have aborted this pregnancy or any other, I declined the sonogram. However, I did contact the cardiologist at Children's Medical Center in Dallas, the cardiologist who had seen Timothy, to make plans to check the baby's heart as soon as possible after birth.

I delivered Daniel by a planned C-section at a hospital in a larger city about an hour away. We had a pediatrician in the delivery room with us to check on the baby immediately, and his exam showed Daniel to be healthy. But we weren't taking any chances. As soon as I was released from the hospital and could ride in the car any distance—when Daniel was about a week old—we took him to the cardiologist at Children's in Dallas for an echocardiogram. Daniel's heart was normal! To say that Bobby and I were thrilled doesn't even begin to describe our relief and gratitude.

Knowing that he had a clean bill of health, we took Daniel home to begin our lives together. But I never completely relaxed until Daniel passed the fourteen-week mark, the age at which we had lost Timothy. I loved Daniel with all my heart and bonded with him in every way that I could. When Daniel turned fifteen weeks old, I finally allowed myself to believe he would really be okay—that Bobby and I would have the chance to be Daniel's parents for the rest of our lives.

About two years after entering the ministry, when Daniel was still a toddler, Bobby realized that this vocation was not for him. The decision-making process was not an easy one. But once we had our direction clear in our hearts, we were at peace and comfortable. In 1989, we moved to Houston to begin the next phase of our family's life.

Bobby took a job in the computer industry, and I went to work as a secretary at Baylor College of Medicine in Houston's enormous medical complex. That's when I fell in love with the healthcare field and began my lifelong passion to contribute in any way that I could. Before long, I became the assistant to one of the top emergency medicine physicians at Ben Taub General Hospital, one of the busiest trauma centers in the country. I absolutely loved that work and would probably still be there today if Bobby's job hadn't transferred us to Dallas.

Bobby and I knew we wanted to have another child after Daniel. Unfortunately, I was having issues again with irregular periods—and this time, it was not due to pregnancy. So after our move to Houston, I began working with a fertility specialist. We did everything—tests, hormones, pretty much everything short of in vitro fertilization. The doctor even brought that up as a last resort, but I told him I wasn't interested. I do believe that life begins at conception, and I could not consider fertilizing eggs that were just going to be thrown away. I also wasn't willing to be implanted with a large number of embryos. So we concluded that in vitro just wasn't something we would pursue.

Before long, Bobby and I realized we needed to "call it quits" and accept our family exactly as it was. God gave us a complete sense of peace with just having Timothy and Daniel—and we have never looked back to second guess our decisions.

When I was pregnant with Daniel, my friends and family might have hoped I was carrying a girl, but the truth is that Daniel looked exactly like Timothy as an infant—and both of them looked exactly like my husband's baby pictures. In fact, when Daniel was a little boy, we had to explain that not all of the framed baby pictures in our house were of him, even though they all looked pretty much the same. That's how we introduced him to Timothy—his older brother who lives in heaven now. We talked about Timothy a lot and have always kept his presence alive in our family in every way we could. During the nine years we lived in Houston, Bobby and Daniel and I visited Timothy's grave on his birthday every year to celebrate his life.

We always brought balloons and pinwheels to decorate the grave, along with little toys, things little boys would enjoy.

When Daniel was a young child, he processed the information about an older brother who had passed away as well as he could. We presented that information to him within the context of our faith, of course, and I know that made it easier for him to understand and accept, as it did for us. But as Daniel became older, we watched him sometimes struggle to answer the inevitable question as to whether or not he had any siblings.

"I'm an only child." That's the answer he would give someone just in passing, someone he didn't have any real relationship with.

But if he were beginning a real friendship with someone, or certainly if it were a young lady he might be interested in, he'd described his situation more fully by saying, "My parents had another son before me, but he's in heaven now. I'm the only child my parents got to raise."

Because of Timothy, I know I've been a different mother to Daniel than I would have been otherwise. Daniel and I have always been very close emotionally. In our family, we don't take one moment for granted because we *know* we are not promised the next day. I know many people are familiar with that concept. They've read about it or studied it in church. But I don't think there's anything in life that could bring that point home more powerfully than losing a child. You just never look at life again with a take-it-for-granted attitude. You no longer have that luxury—or that ignorance.

Daniel is twenty-five years old now, a college graduate and a U.S. Army lieutenant in air defense artillery. So he is clearly a very strong and independent young man! But toward me, he is absolutely tender-hearted—and always has been. It was clear that, as a child, he took special care of me because of the pain of my loss. He just did everything he could for me. And as he grew, that sensitive nature just blossomed into a wonderful part of his total personality. Daniel still calls me every night to say goodnight, just to check in. I might not need that kind of care from him right now, but I'll admit I love it. The fact that he still sees our relationship as such a priority in his life is just incredible to me. I also have to give my husband credit, of course. Bobby is a wonderful and attentive son to his own mother, and Daniel certainly sees that example.

Daniel was nine years old when we moved to Dallas from Houston. For two years, I stayed home with him while we built a house and settled into our new life. When I did go back to work, I worked in telecommunications and banking for the first several years. I certainly wanted to go back to healthcare, but Dallas geography just didn't quite work out for me. The city's medical school and main medical complex were on the other side of town from where we lived, and I just wasn't comfortable being that far from Daniel. The city's telecom corridor, on the other hand, was right down the street. If I needed to run up to his school for anything, I could do it easily.

It was during this period that I heard of Dr. Nikaidoh's tragic loss of his own son, Dr. Hitoshi Nikaidoh. I hadn't seen or spoken to Dr. Nikaidoh since immediately after Timothy's death seventeen years earlier. But my heart just broke for this man who had given so very much to so many families.

Losing a child is a unique experience that sets you apart from the rest of the world. For a parent to bury a child is absolutely the most unnatural thing in this life. That is *not* the way it is supposed to happen according to every dream you've ever had, every image about the future that might have passed through your thoughts. Your children are supposed to bury you.

On the other hand, having lost a child equips you to be one of the few who can comfort others walking that path. No one else knows what they are going through. But you do. When you say that you know their pain, that you understand, the newly grieving parent knows you mean it.

So Bobby and I reached out to comfort Dr. Nikaidoh in the way he had comforted us. The letter he had sent us all those years earlier still contained the precious words that had brought a measure of comfort to our hearts: "I can only pray for you that the warm love of our Lord will fill the painful void in your heart leading you to the healing from this hurt in His time. Please remember my prayers are with you." We sent those exact words back to him now, hoping and praying to bring a bit of peace to *his* grieving heart. He had cared so deeply about us in our time of need. We wanted him to know that we cared just as deeply about him in his.

In 2006, Daniel was away at college, and I was ready to go back to work across town in the healthcare field. I applied to several places, including Children's Medical Center. I'll admit I was nervous to go back to the building where we had held Timothy for the very last time, the place where he had passed away. But as soon as I walked in for the interview, I felt fine. The building had been remodeled since we had been there, to the extent that I hardly recognized a thing. That's what saved me.

For the past six years, I have worked as executive assistant to the president and CEO of Children's, and I absolutely love it. My job is different every single day. There is always a challenge, always a new skill to learn and apply. I'm not providing direct care to the children, but I know I am a cog in that wheel. By helping those in administration to be the right place at the right time, I'm helping support those who do provide direct care. The hospital has grown and increased its outreach so much while I've been here, and I am so proud to have been even a tiny part of that good work.

Unlike so many families who bring their children to this hospital over a period of years, our interaction was only a matter of hours. And yet, coming to work here felt like coming home. There are certainly days when I am very well aware that my baby died right here in this building. But even on those days— or maybe especially on those days—I choose to focus on the hope that the work in this hospital brings to so many. I just can't imagine any job more wonderful than working with this enormous team to "make life better for children" and their families – our mission at Children's.

I like to think that even if Timothy had been perfectly

healthy, even if God had allowed us to keep him for a natural lifetime, I would still be a sensitive, helpful person who could empathize with others. But as I walk through the halls of this hospital every day, I know that I have something unique to give because of the loss of Timothy.

There are times when I share with a family the fact that I have walked in their shoes, that I have come full circle right here in this building. And the empathy, the tiny bit of peace that I can give them is something not many people can offer. I wouldn't be able to offer it either, if it hadn't been for Timothy.

And the God of all grace, who called you to his eternal glory in Christ, after you have suffered a little while, will himself restore you and make you strong, firm, and steadfast.

1 Peter 5:10
New International Version

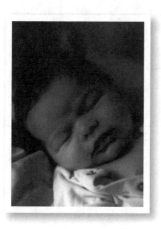

Timothy Dick

CHAPTER 9

LIZ ETZKORN

In the autumn of 1988, an infant girl was brought to Children's on the verge of death. She had a heart condition so rare—complex double outlet right ventricle with coarctation of the aorta—that even today, the vast majority of physicians wouldn't be able to describe it to you. By the time we saw her, she was in shock due to inadequate blood flow to the body's tissues. I knew what to do to give her the best chance for survival right then and there. But as a mere human, and given the state of medicine almost a quarter of a century ago, I could not foresee the future of this beautiful little girl.

I WAS EIGHTEEN YEARS OLD when I met Tom Etzkorn, and it was absolutely love at first sight for me. I had just graduated from high school in my tiny hometown of Dierks, Arkansas. Like most of my classmates, I had gone to work in the town's lumber mill. Tom was my supervisor. At twenty-five, he was an "older man" with the most beautiful blue eyes I had ever seen. We were married just over a year after we met, and our first child, Brian, was born the following year.

I was thrilled to have started my family at such a young age.

True, I'd had some other dreams when I was younger. I'd always said I wanted to be a nurse. But once I met Tom, nothing was more important to me than starting my family. Whenever I imagined my future, I would see myself as a grandmother surrounded by a large and loving family. I was so happy with Tom and Brian that I never looked back.

When Brian was two years old, we moved to Commerce, Texas, for Tom to take a job after the mill fell on hard times, and I decided to open a childcare business in our home. It was a wonderful arrangement. I could be with Brian during the day, take care of other children, and earn money all at the same time. The following year, our son Joshua was born. I was as content as could be with my two boys and all my daycare children.

Then about three years later, we decided to have one more child. Another boy would have been fine, of course. But I really wanted to try for a little girl. I knew this would be my last child—in fact, I had decided to have a tubal ligation immediately after this baby's birth. With three children, Tom and I would have the perfect size family. And when you added in my daycare babies, I knew my hands would be full!

On October 21, 1988, at the end of a long and difficult labor, I heard the words I had been hoping for: "It's a girl. A healthy baby girl!" Brooke Elizabeth was so tiny, so precious, so perfect. I could not have been happier. My family was now complete, and I had a tubal ligation as planned the following morning.

When Brooke was about ten days old, she began breathing a little heavy and seemed to be coming down with a cold. Three days later, her breathing became more labored, and she stopped nursing. As a third-time parent, I had seen many illnesses come and go over the years. But I wasn't sure what medication to give a newborn to keep her comfortable during a cold. So I took her to the pediatrician.

The doctor examined her, listening carefully to her chest. Then he said the words that would change my life forever.

"Mrs. Etzkorn, your little girl doesn't have a cold. She has heart problems. She could have any of these five things wrong with her," he said as he scribbled notes on the paper covering the exam table. "Or, she could have all five. She needs to be seen by a cardiologist. Today."

What in the world was he talking about? Ventricles? Aorta? Blockage?

I was near hysterics when I called Tom. We drove together to the cardiologist in Dallas. The doctor weighed Brooke and did an electrocardiogram to look at her heartbeat. Then he asked me to put her in my lap facing him, and he felt all around her chest and heart.

He left the room for a few minutes, and when he came back in, he gave us instructions I will never forget. "I want you to leave here now and drive directly to Children's Medical Center. Do not stop anywhere along the way for *any* reason. You don't have to speed. But you do need to drive straight there to the Emergency Room. They're waiting for you."

I sat in the backseat holding my little princess all the way there, tears running down my face as I prayed to God to help her get better.

When we pulled up to the Emergency entrance, a man came right over and asked if we were the Etzkorns. He led me inside with Brooke, who was pale and weak by this time, while Tom went to park the car. Several doctors and nurses huddling together took Brooke from me and walked into another room. As they carried her away, I heard one of them say, "She's just gone into shock."

And there I was, alone.

When Tom came in, Dr. Nikaidoh introduced himself and led us into a room to talk. He began to tell us about Brooke's problems.

"Your daughter is a very sick little girl," Dr. Nikaidoh told us. "She has four major problems with her heart. Her heart itself isn't built right. She's missing a wall between two of the pumping chambers. She has too much blood rushing to her lungs. In another place, she has a blockage. We can't fix all of these today. But if we don't get in there and do what we can, she will die."

Dr. Nikaidoh was very kind and patient with us, but it was too much for us to take in all at one time. We couldn't concentrate at all until he came to the last statement. *That* we understood: If our baby did not have heart surgery that very day, she would die.

We gave permission, signed all the papers, met with surgeons, anesthesiologists, doctors from the Intensive Care Unit, social workers, chaplains—all in one day, all in one tearful and terrifying blur.

Eventually, they let us go see Brooke in the ICU. She had tubes in her mouth, each hand, and both legs. Her beautiful brownish red hair had been shaved, and she had an IV in her head. She just lay there looking lifeless. That was the absolute worst thing I had ever seen in my life. All I could do was kiss her, stroke her little arms and legs, and tell her how much I loved her and wanted her to fight for her life.

Had I really taken my precious girl to the pediatrician just that very morning for what I thought was a cold?

They took Brooke down to the operating room at about nine o'clock that night, and just after midnight, Dr. Nikaidoh came out to tell us that the surgery had gone well. At least for now, Brooke's partially blocked segment of aorta was repaired, and the dangerous rush of blood to the lungs was controlled by a band on the main pulmonary artery. We knew she would need more surgeries in the future. But we didn't have to think about that. And we didn't want to. At her two-week post-surgical check-up, everything looked fine.

Brooke turned two months old the week of her first Christmas. We put her in a beautiful red dress with a bow in her hair. She absolutely looked like a little doll. We spent a wonderful holiday with our whole family. She was smiling and cooing, and had started kicking those tiny little legs back and forth, back and forth. She was just adorable, and her brothers were so proud of their baby sister. All through the following spring, summer, and fall, Brooke did well. We continued to go to the cardiologist for check-ups every three months—and all the news was good.

Tom and I enjoyed and marveled at the development of each

of our babies. But with Brooke, every milestone during that year felt like a miracle. We watched her learn to roll on the floor, drag herself, crawl, and use her scooter to get into every single cabinet in the kitchen. She started standing up in her crib and then walking. We did notice that she tired out more easily than our boys had at her age, but we didn't think it was anything to worry about.

Before we knew it, we were celebrating a double birthday—Brooke and her little cousin born three days after her both reaching their first birthdays. We had pink plates, pink napkins, and pink hats for the birthday girls! Tom and I gave her a swing, which she spent many happy hours in. Brian and Josh gave her a baby doll that Brian had purchased with his own money, and Brooke absolutely loved it. We all had a great day adoring our happy little girl.

But over the next two months, as I noticed Brooke tiring more and more easily, I did become concerned. Just before Christmas, we had to switch to a new cardiologist because of changes in our insurance plan. At our first visit with the new doctor, I told her Brooke definitely was not as active as she had been just a few months before.

The doctor said Brooke's heart was working so hard—which was one of the reasons she also had such a difficult time gaining weight—that she thought it might be time for her next surgery to give her heart some relief.

I was shocked. I was worried about Brooke's lack of energy, but I thought we'd have several more years before we'd have to face another surgery. Yes, Brooke had made it through that first surgery so well. But what if it were different this time? What if there were complications?

The doctor said she would speak to all the cardiologists and surgeons on Brooke's team at Children's to come to a consensus. Three weeks later, she told me they felt it wasn't time yet for surgery, and I felt a great sense of relief.

But this is where the mistakes began.

I believe now that Brooke *should* have had the surgery at that time. Or at least a cardiac catheterization to find out exactly what was going on with her heart. Or at the very least, she should have been seen by the doctor every few weeks to check her progress. Instead, the cardiologist said she didn't need to see Brooke back for three months. Three whole months.

As it turned out, we couldn't wait that long.

Within a few weeks, I called the cardiologist to say that Brooke was tiring even more easily now. By seven o'clock in the evening, she would be completely exhausted and lethargic. Sometimes, she would toddle over to the couch, lay her little head on the seat cushion, and shut her eyes and rest.

"Mrs. Etzkorn, you know Brooke just started walking a few months ago. Walking is using up all her energy. I think it makes sense that she's worn out by evening," the doctor said. But it didn't make sense to me. I had raised two other babies and I *knew* this wasn't normal. I knew this was more than just "using up her energy."

A few weeks later, I was even more concerned. Brooke had stopped gaining weight and was lethargic *all* the time. I called the cardiologist again, but the receptionist said none of the six doctors in that office could see us that day.

I was furious! I could not believe that no one in that office could make room for their own patient when she was clearly in distress. But I didn't have any time to waste in arguing with them. I called her original cardiology practice and got Brooke in the next day.

After running an electrocardiogram on her, the new doctor told Tom and me that Brooke needed to have a cardiac catheterization, an invasive test. He must have seen the look of panic on my face. I was so worried about them putting something into my baby's heart.

"I understand that you'd rather Brooke not have an invasive test," he said. "But we have to know what's happening inside her heart. We cannot continue to play a guessing game."

The catheterization was performed at Children's Medical Center, and everything went well. But when the cardiologist took

Tom and me in to show us the test results, we were devastated. What we saw on the test was nothing like what we had imagined. All along, we thought that Brooke's heart had the two ventricles, the two pumping chambers, just as she was supposed to—but that the left one wasn't functioning very well. What we saw from that test was that she only had a nub for her left ventricle. The doctor explained that it was hardly formed at all because of the narrowing of the hole between the two ventricles. I honestly didn't know what all that meant at the time. All I knew was that for the first time, I could *see* how poorly formed my baby's heart was.

The cardiologist explained Brooke needed two surgical repairs: There was one issue with the heart itself and another issue with the right pulmonary artery, which was now partially blocked by the band they had put in during her first surgery.

We checked in to the hospital the day before her surgery and met with the assistant surgeon who told us exactly what they planned to do.

"Is that all?" I asked when he had finished. "What about her right pulmonary artery? You didn't mention it. The cardiologist told us that was one of the most important issues."

"What?" The doctor looked confused and started flipping through the pages of Brooke's chart. I felt a terrible wave of panic rising up in me. Did I know more about Brooke's heart than this surgeon did?

"I need to see Dr. Nikaidoh," I said, standing up. "Please. Can you just get Dr. Nikaidoh for me?" I was upset and knew it showed, but I didn't care.

Dr. Nikaidoh wore a certain type of shoes in those days, a type of clog that made a unique noise coming down the hall. I had come to associate the sound of his footsteps with a feeling of comfort because I knew I would be getting the help I needed. But this time I was angry and worried. I practically jumped on him as soon as I heard his footsteps.

"What's going on? Why didn't the other surgeon know about the pulmonary artery? What's wrong?" I was close to tears.

Dr. Nikaidoh walked over to check on Brooke and then

turned back to me. "Mrs. Etzkorn, I apologize that my associate did not know about the pulmonary artery. I am very well aware of that issue, and he should have been too. And I really do hate to tell you this news, but we have to delay the surgery. The catheterization shows us only Brooke's right pulmonary artery, but not the left. We have to have another catheterization."

"What? The new cardiologist didn't do the right test? The test we just put her through was a waste of time?" By then I was crying.

"I am so sorry. But we have to have this additional information before surgery," Dr. Nikaidoh said. "I understand this must be so hard for you."

"Yes it's hard for me," I cried. "But it's harder for Brooke."

We had no choice, so we left the hospital to wait until we could schedule the test. When I got home, I settled Brooke in, and then I went straight to church. I knew God would understand my feelings. I knew I could count on Him to make my baby better.

When we finally checked back into Children's, and she had her additional catheterization—a week later than we had hoped because Brooke had developed a rash, and we had to wait for that to clear up—the cardiologist gave us more bad news. He had not been able to thread the catheter through to the left pulmonary artery. It just wouldn't go. So the test had given us *no* additional information. The surgery postponement and Brooke's suffering through one more test had all been for nothing.

I was so anxious to see Dr. Nikaidoh that day. I knew he would come talk to us because Brooke's surgery was scheduled for the following morning. He was the one doctor I could count on to be calm and compassionate and really take time with all my questions—a source of strength for me at so many anxious times. I listened all day for the sound of his shoes in the hallway, but he never showed up. Every time I asked the nurses where he was, they said he was in surgery. Finally, at 10:30 in the evening, I heard his footsteps.

"I am so sorry to be coming up so late," he said. "I have been in surgery with the same child the entire day. In fact, I have to go back and continue the surgery now." He paused for a moment before continuing, "Mrs. Etzkorn, the only reason I left the operating room was so I could tell you personally that I will not be able to do Brooke's surgery in the morning."

I was so exhausted that I thought maybe I had misunderstood. "What?"

"I am so sorry. But I expect to be in surgery well into the early morning hours. I just cannot operate on Brooke without getting some rest. It would be too dangerous. So I'm afraid we will have to postpone for one week."

"No! No, we can't do that. Why is that other child more important than my baby? Brooke is getting weaker every day, and I've been telling everyone that for months. But no one has time for her!" I was in tears, crying from frustration and exhaustion. I could see on Dr. Nikaidoh's face that he was genuinely torn and troubled by the situation. But I kept pushing and pushing because my baby needed help, and that was all I cared about. "It's been one mistake and problem after the next. Why is this happening? Dr. Nikaidoh, you have to help her."

He looked over at Brooke in the bed for a minute while I blew my nose and wiped my tears. Then he asked, "Is that how she normally breathes?"

I looked at her too. "Yes."

Dr. Nikaidoh watched her for another moment and then turned back to me. "No, we won't wait an entire week. I'll do her surgery on Saturday, in two days."

"Thank you. Thank you so much." I prayed for Brooke that night, adding a prayer for the other child Dr. Nikaidoh was working so hard to save.

Brooke's surgery, the day before Easter, lasted about five hours. Afterward, Dr. Nikaidoh told us there had been some problems, but that she was stable. What we learned later was that Brooke's heart had functioned very poorly in the operating room, barely pumping enough blood to her body's tissues. Without adequate oxygen delivery, the brain, kidneys, and liver all begin to fail. And in fact, Brooke never regained consciousness after her surgery. When I went into the ICU to see her, my precious girl had tubes in both nostrils, needles in each arm and foot, and monitors everywhere. I had never felt more helpless in my life. Easter Sunday was a very difficult day. The previous year we had dressed her up so cute, and she had been doing so well. It had been such a wonderful holiday for the whole family. My sister had already bought Brooke her Easter dress for this year. I couldn't dress her in it, but the nurses let me lay it on top of her, on top of all her tubes and wires. And I put a little bow in her hair.

Brooke started running a fever, and her liver and kidney function slowly declined. Then she began to have seizures. I spent my days praying, rubbing cream on her eyelids and lips because they were so dry, and listening for the sound of Dr. Nikaidoh's footsteps in the hallway.

On Thursday night, five days after her surgery, when all the family except Tom and me had gone home or to their hotels, I went back into the ICU to see Brooke one more time that day. The nurse by her bed turned toward me.

"Mrs. Etzkorn, would you like to help me give Brooke a bath?"

"Oh my goodness. I would absolutely love that." I had tears in my eyes. "But how could I do it without hurting her—I mean, with all those tubes and everything?"

Those nurses showed us so much compassion that night, as always—in the way they held Brooke, the way they handled her tubes or stroked her head with the gentlest of hands, how they welcomed me into the process of her care, the fact that they never lost patience with my questions. I was always grateful for their extraordinary kindness, but never more grateful than that night. I fixed her beautiful silky hair and put her little Easter bow back in. I sang to her, kissed her, and told her to be a big girl and keep on fighting. I rubbed those precious fingers and kissed those soft cheeks. And, of course, I cried.

When I went in to see Brooke the next morning, the right side of her body was swollen and hard. Later that afternoon, her forehead felt almost cold to the touch. Dr. Nikaidoh came back in while I was there, and I told him about her forehead. I watched him while he checked Brooke all over and looked at all the monitors. Then he stared at Brooke in her bed. When he looked up and met my eyes, I saw it in his face.

He asked me to gather Tom and our brothers and sisters who were there with us, and he took us into the family room. Our church family and friends waited outside.

"We have done everything we can for Brooke, but her brain cells are dying. Brooke will never recover," Dr. Nikaidoh said. He spoke slowly and quietly, wiping tears from his eyes. "I wish I could tell you something different. We could run more tests, but it wouldn't be fair to her. Brooke's soul has already left. Only the machines are keeping her body alive."

We all cried, and Dr. Nikaidoh cried with us. Then he wiped his eyes again, took a deep breath, and looked at Tom and me. "I think it's time to allow her to go," he said. "We'll need to unhook her from the machines."

"All right."

Who said that? Who gave permission for the doctors and nurses to move out of the way of Brooke's death? It was my voice. But I could never, ever have given permission to take my baby off those life-giving machines. It was God's grace that freed Brooke that day. Not me.

Somehow, we stood up and walked back into the ICU. The nurses took all her tubes and IV lines out and brought Brooke into another room. I sat in a rocking chair, and they placed her in my arms. Brian came in, and somehow God gave me the strength to explain to him about his baby sister. Then I sang "Hush, Little Baby" to Brooke—like I always had. Tom took her into his arms to hold his baby girl one last time and then gave her back to me. When the nurses took her pacemaker and ventilator off, she passed away in my arms.

I wanted to cry, cry and scream, and hold her little body for hours. And looking back, I wish I *had* done exactly that. But instead, I held her just a little longer and struggled to be strong for my family. I laid her back on the bed. I kissed her and told her that Mama loved her forever. Then I turned and walked out of that room, leaving my baby and my dreams of my daughter forever on earth.

After her funeral, I closed down my daycare business. I just couldn't spend that much time at home, and all the parents understood. I spent a lot of my time crying, day and night. Brian cried a lot too. He was eight years old when Brooke died and had been big enough to carry her around. He missed that baby sister so much. Josh, who was five at that time, went from being a big brother to being a baby again, and he did not know how to express his grief at this tender age. In bed at night, Tom and I would cry and pray together.

There are no words that could possibly describe the depth of my pain that first year after Brooke's death. It was worse than any pain I had ever felt in my life, worse than any pain I had ever even imagined. Without God's grace and love, I honestly believe I would have died too.

We had the support of my family, Tom's family, and the church family, and I can't imagine what we would have done without them. But they could not lessen my pain. I knew they sincerely wanted to help me feel better, but nothing made any difference. For a while, I tried reading books about grief. I forced myself to believe that if I just read every book I could find about grief, I would feel better when I read the last page. I was wrong.

Occasionally during that first year, family and friends would try to console me by pointing out that I still had two healthy children. They told me to focus on them. Of course, I knew I was blessed, and I loved and appreciated my precious Brian and Josh. I thanked God for them every single day. But people didn't seem to understand that having the boys couldn't take away the pain of losing Brooke! It's like people who have lost a limb: If they still have three others, they'll be grateful, but they are always going to miss the limb they lost. That's how it was with me. When I lost Brooke, I lost a part of myself.

Here's the truth: We have to grieve. There is only the grief and each person's way of working through it. Grief works on its own timetable, and it is only with God's love and grace that any of us moves forward.

God did bring something to me that truly helped. Not long after Brooke's death, Tom and I heard about a bereavement support group at Children's, and we decided to try it. Tom went just that one time; being in that group setting just did not feel right to him. But for me, that group became a lifeline. For one evening each month, I would be with people who truly knew what I was going through. For one evening, I didn't have to pretend I was keeping everything together. For just that one group of people—parents who had lost a child—I didn't have to worry that the depth of my pain was making them uncomfortable. They knew that same pain.

I learned so much from that bereavement group. Most importantly, I learned that I was not going crazy. I learned that other parents cried as much as I did. They, too, hugged, smelled, and slept with their children's clothes. Some of the parents had gone to lay down in graveyards to be as close as possible to what remained of their child on this earth. It was a real relief to be assured that I wasn't "losing my mind." I also learned how blessed I was to have Tom. I discovered that some fathers never talked about their child who had passed away. They would never mention the child's name or refer to the loss in any way. I don't know how those mothers made it through without that support.

With the emotional support of the group and everyone else I loved, but mostly with God's love and grace, I made it through that first year. On the anniversary of Brooke's death, I felt that I had to go back to the ICU, to the last place I had held her in my arms. I just had to be there. The rooms were filled with parents and children I didn't know. But the ICU itself felt familiar, and I felt a closeness to Brooke.

I went up to the ICU again on the second anniversary of her death for the same reason. Again, I felt that special closeness. This time, I heard the familiar footsteps and saw Dr. Nikaidoh down the hallway. I walked up to him.

"Dr. Nikaidoh, you probably don't remember me ..." I started.

"Of course I remember you," he interrupted. "You're Brooke's mother."

I could tell he was surprised to see me at the hospital but wasn't sure what to say. So I explained, "Today is the anniversary of her death, Dr. Nikaidoh. She has been gone for two full years. I feel close to her here somehow."

"I am so sorry for your loss. I truly am," he said.

And I knew he meant it. Only six days after Brooke's death, Tom and I received a handwritten note of condolence from Dr. Nikaidoh. We were so touched that he had taken the time from his extremely busy schedule to express his compassion with such beautiful and meaningful words, letting us know that he was praying for us and remembering Brooke. His words were such a powerful comfort to us. Each year, on Brooke's birthday and on the anniversary of her death, I wrote Dr. Nikaidoh a note, thanking him for using his God-given gifts in the surgery that allowed Brooke to be with us for those eighteen months. Each time, I would receive a handwritten note back from him. Again, he would express his memories of her and his compassion for us as we continue our journey without her.

I don't think Dr. Nikaidoh will ever know the comfort and the healing that each of those notes brought to Tom and me. God certainly blessed him with wonderful talents to allow him to surgically mend those tiny hearts. But He gave him an even greater gift to comfort the parents of those whose little hearts were not meant to be mended.

Soon after meeting Dr. Nikaidoh in the hospital, when I had been going to the bereavement group for about two years, I started to feel a change in myself. I wouldn't say there was a big difference. But I would call it a significant difference. I began to realize that I would survive. I knew I would live through this, something I wasn't so sure of at first. But now I knew. So after two years, as the bereavement group just naturally started dwindling down a bit, I too stopped going.

During the time I was attending the group—in fact just about six months after Brooke's death—I had taken a job as the receptionist at a veterinarian's office. I initially took the job just because I had to do something since closing my childcare business, but what a blessing it turned out to be! Everyone at the clinic knew about my situation and was so supportive of me. And the vet was practically a comedian. You never knew from one day to the next what prank he was going to pull. That place was just such great medicine for me. It gave me something I desperately needed—something to laugh about. I could not have chosen a more wonderful place to work.

It was during my employment at the vet clinic that I made the decision to go to nursing school. Actually, it wasn't like a decision that I *made*. It was more like a realization that I came to. I began to understand that I was born to be a nurse. This is what I was meant to do. I just knew.

When I told Tom, he was concerned about the timing. He wondered if it were a good idea to make such a big decision in the middle of so much grief and turmoil. But he supported me all the way. The vet allowed me to be very flexible with my work schedule, so I started taking nursing prerequisites at a local university—just one class per semester at the beginning.

I was on my way.

I'll be honest: School was much harder than I had imagined. Not only had I never attended college—and here I was in my early thirties—but I was still so deep in my grief that I could barely concentrate. Some days, I felt like everything just zipped right by me with very little actually sinking into my brain. Between work, school, and caring for the boys and family, I was almost always exhausted. But as hard as it was, I knew I had to get through this if I wanted to be a nurse. So I did.

It took a good long while to finish all the prerequisites and be accepted into nursing school. But before I started that part of my education, there was one more thing I wanted to do first. I wanted to try to have another child. It was never my intention to try to replace Brooke. I was clear about that. But I did want to have another child. Tom agreed, and so I had my tubal ligation surgically reversed. I did become pregnant, but I miscarried at six weeks. I became pregnant again, but this time it was a tubal pregnancy. After everything I had been through, God's love and grace helped me face the loss of those two pregnancies. I realized it was time for me to accept the fact that I was not meant to have any more children. I was at peace with it.

The semester I began nursing school, I quit my job at the vet—although I hated to leave everyone there—because I knew nursing school would require my full-time commitment. And I was right. The quantity and difficulty of the work was astounding. On my good days, it felt overwhelming, and on my bad days, I thought I'd never get through it. But somehow, I did make it through. After my very last day of nursing school, I pulled into our home driveway to see Brian and Josh standing there waiting for me with a big homemade sign. The sign read, "Welcome Home, Million Dollar Nurse Mom!" I hope they didn't really think I was going to become a millionaire! But I did become a registered nurse, and it made me feel just wonderful that they were so proud and supportive.

I started out working in a hospital and then moved to home health. But my schedules at both places were horrible, and I missed way too much of family life, church, and the boys' weekend activities. So I took a job as an occupational-health nurse at a large defense contractor. This wasn't the job I had imagined when I went to nursing school. But the hours—Monday through Friday, 8 a.m. to 5 p.m.—qualified it as my "dream job" at that time in my life. I worked there for nine years.

In 2003, we moved thirty minutes away in order to build a house. I wanted to work closer to home, so I quit my position and went to look for a part-time nursing job in hospice care in Sulphur Springs, our new town. I had never worked in that field or even had a friend in hospice. But I just knew in my heart that I could bring so much to people facing the end of life. The local hospital wasn't looking for anyone right then, but I went downstairs to the hospice department anyway.

"I realize there aren't any openings right now," I told the director. "I just wanted to introduce myself and let you know I'm looking for something part-time."

"It's funny that you should walk in the door right this minute," the woman said to me. "I've been thinking about hiring someone part-time, but I hadn't advertised it yet. Would you be interested in interviewing?"

And there it was—hospice, the job I was meant for. Hospice nursing is the most satisfying work I've ever done in my life, the reason I went to nursing school, and Brooke's legacy—all wrapped up into one. Yes, there are some sad and difficult times. But I can honestly say that hospice brings me more joy than I could have imagined. This is the work I was created for.

What could be more important than providing comfort—physical, emotional, and even spiritual comfort—at this unique moment in life? I love knowing that I'm making such a difference. And I love helping my patients identify what they want to accomplish with the time they have left.

"How would you like to use this time? Is there something you have wanted to do that we could help you achieve?" I always ask.

One of my patients wanted to have his whole family come together for a meal. So we made that happen—and what a wonderful memory for everyone. Another patient wanted to go to a movie that would make him laugh. So we arranged for a showing of a completely silly movie at a local theater, and we just laughed and laughed. That's all this patient asked for, and we were honored to grant him this last request.

But the most special part of hospice work for me has been being with my patients when they die. They've gone through so much suffering, and death is such a peaceful time in comparison. All they need from me at that point is to just be there and love them, and it is my honor to do exactly that.

In addition to my hospice work, about seven years ago I started a monthly support group at my church, League Street Church of Christ, for parents who have lost a child at my church. I had wanted to start it years earlier because I knew how much the grief group at Children's helped me. But the truth is that it took me years before I could comfortably share my own story. So I waited until God gave me the strength to support these parents. I wanted to call the group something that was related to Brooke without actually using her name. I decided on "In the Heart of a Parent." After all, our children might not be here with us any longer, but they are always in our hearts.

Although we started out with about ten people at that first meeting, some of them didn't come back. Sharing your pain and loss in a group setting is not for everyone, and I never measure the group's success based on numbers. If only one person comes to a particular meeting, then I know God knew I needed to be with that one person that night. That's my blessing.

I love offering support for those parents. But I'll admit it's difficult for me when someone's loss is recent and I can just feel the crushing intensity of his or her pain. About six years ago, my own sister lost her adult son, Shane, and I felt so helpless in trying to comfort her. I wish I could have moved her and the other parents ten years down the road. I want to assure them that the pain will lessen eventually, that they will feel happiness again one day. But only God can move the time forward. I just do what I can. And of course, the group has provided continued comfort for me as well.

All of us need support from time to time, throughout our lives. I remember Josh coming home from college one day and calling me upstairs to his room. I could tell something was wrong. When I asked him what was bothering him, he said he was angry—really, really angry.

"Mom, why did Brooke have to die? Why?" And my twenty-year-old son burst into tears. I just took him and held him in my arms. Josh was practically a baby himself when Brooke died. Now as he moves forward into the world as a man, it makes sense that he is grieving her loss again, this time as an adult. I could certainly understand his questions of "why?"

I too still have difficult, painful times even after so many years. When Brooke had been gone for quite a few years, I learned that

Children's Medical Center was going through a major renovation and was abandoning the ICU where we had been. I had such a strong reaction to that news. I just had to drive back to Dallas to "feel" her there one last time before they rebuilt that space into something I wouldn't recognize. All the patients and families had already been moved to the new area, and the old ICU area was off limits but, thankfully, no one stopped me on my way up. I stepped off the elevator into a stunning and complete silence. The floor had always been filled with such urgency, so much movement and sound. But now, just emptiness. I slowly found my way back to the room where I had last held Brooke. In the complete quiet, I could feel her presence.

"Mama loves you, Brooke," I told her that day. "And my precious baby girl, I'm glad you aren't suffering anymore."

I stood for a while longer and then walked through those halls one last time. A security guard was on the elevator when I stepped in, but he didn't say anything to me. I'm sure he could tell I'd been crying.

Just recently, Brooke's legacy in this world was made clear in a very public way. I recently started working in a new position as director of hospice care for Hopkins County Memorial Hospital in Sulphur Springs. I'll still have the opportunity to provide some patient care, but I'll also be setting the tone and direction for the hospital's hospice program. I was introduced to the board of directors by one of the local physicians—whose granddaughter had also been a patient of Dr. Nikaidoh's—and he told them about my background, specifically mentioning Brooke.

"Who better to direct our hospice program? Who better than a nurse who knows first-hand what it means to suffer the loss of a child?" he said.

And there it was—Brooke's legacy just put out there for everyone to see. Because the truth is that her life and death made me who I am today to a very great extent. Maybe I would have eventually followed my childhood dream into nursing in any case. Maybe. But I know I would not have become the quality nurse I am today, someone who so deeply understands and respects the needs of the dying and their families—someone who is capable of giving so much love at such a crucial and holy time.

Tom and the boys and I live Brooke's legacy every day, as we recognize the value of life and the precious nature of every moment in a way many other people don't. We *know* first-hand that there is no guarantee of a tomorrow here on earth. In fact, our whole extended family has come together with an even deeper and more demonstrable love than before. "I love you" is a phrase we say right out loud all the time now to make sure no one is left wondering about their place in this family's heart. And ever since my son Brian and his wife gave us our first grandchild two years ago—our precious granddaughter, Autumn Brooke—you can be sure we all give that child all the love anyone could need every single day. Josh and his wife are expecting their first child, and that baby too will be showered with love.

By far the biggest lesson I learned from Brooke's life and death is this: God is in control. Not me, but God.

When Brooke was alive and struggling, I just prayed my heart out for her, and I was absolutely sure God would answer my prayers in exactly the way I wanted them answered. I knew that if I could just pray hard enough and be a good enough Christian, then God would heal Brooke. The God I believed in back then just would not allow my daughter to die.

But as God has helped me mature in my faith through the past twenty-plus years since I lost her, I've learned that no matter what I pray for, only God truly knows what's for the best. Instead of trying to be in control of what God does, I need to be at peace with His decisions. Not that it's easy! It is not. But God knows that too.

Over time, I have been able to see and appreciate so many positive things in this world that have come from Brooke's life—and even from her death. But I know now that God's plan is way beyond anything I can see on this earth. He is in charge. He knows what's best. And for that, I am truly grateful. Brooke is no longer here with me, but she is forever in my heart.

But when you fully own your pain and do not expect those to whom you minister to alleviate it, you can speak about it in true freedom. Then sharing your struggle can become a service; then your openness about yourself can offer courage and hope to others.

The Inner Voice of Love,
Henri J. M. Nouwen,
Image Books, Doubleday, 1998

Brooke Elizabeth Etzkorn

EPILOGUE

Although the mothers profiled in this book have revealed extraordinary courage and strength as they continue to face their journeys of grief and love, they are by no means alone. Each year, tens of thousands of parents in our country are forced to begin that journey as we, too, experience the excruciating pain of losing our precious child. It is a pain that seems to be without end as it burns into our lives. But as these parents have so eloquently shared, it is a pain that we can and do live through, even if we find that scenario difficult to imagine at the time of our loss. It is a pain that does become more manageable as God showers us with His love and grace and sees to it that the days and nights move forward. It is a pain that sometimes lessens a bit when we turn our focus to helping others. It is a pain that will never leave us completely.

It is my hope that we can all learn from the gift given by the parents in this book as they have openly shared the depth of their grief. I hope we can learn how to better walk with a loved one or friend who has suffered such a loss. I hope we can learn to better respect the grieving process itself—so unique to each person in manner and length, as these mothers have revealed. And in the process of grief and the recovery, which is often providential, we should not forget the importance of so many who lend their support—whether spouse, children, parents, or friends. Through this long process of grieving and healing, we can all re-learn the precious nature of our lives.

What have I personally learned from these kind and brave mothers who shared their pain and suffering? I have learned the value of human life far more than any medical school could teach me. More importantly, I have learned the unique value of the very special privilege that is bestowed upon all medical professionals: doctors, nurses, ancillary medical service staff, social workers, and chaplains. That special privilege is the personal relationship between us and the patients who are given into our hands by the providential wisdom of God. We should never handle this unusual privilege carelessly or take it for granted.

As medical professionals, it is often our distorted misconception that death occurs only because we have not provided the correct medical treatment. But the truth is that even with the best medical care, death still occurs! We are all human beings who know the limitation of biological life; we know that death and its subsequent grief are integral parts of life. As we are born, we will die—without question. It is a delusion to blame someone or something for every death.

But what should we do as medical professionals when that inevitable death occurs? Each physician is responsible and obligated to respect the deceased and to extend the most sincere and loving emotional support to the family. This is our appropriate response to the Almighty God who allowed us to take care of this individual, His precious child.

Having acknowledged the inevitability of death and the suffering faced by the family, I also want to acknowledge that as physicians, we work incessantly to promote life so that families will have as much time as possible with their loved ones on this earth. And I am happy to be able to report that medical science has come a long way in the years since many of the children in this book were born.

As a surgeon who has observed the development of congenital heart surgery from its infancy to today over the time span of more than forty years, I can assure you that today's prognosis for many heart conditions is very favorable. It is true that a few of the children in this book were born with such severely deformed hearts that we still might not have much to offer in terms of effective treatment. But for the majority of these children, we would expect much better outcomes for their conditions today. We have learned from our past painful experiences and have continuously improved our performance in both diagnosis and treatment.

But even for those children whom we cannot save from death, we know that death is not the end. As these stories have told us through each mother's mouth, God's redemptive power reaches far beyond our comprehension, and healing will come to all of us as we wait on the Lord. The medical profession will not be able to bring a physical cure to all patients, but God is not limited and will provide what we need.

Praise be to God whose love and mercy endure forever.

He will wipe away every tear from their eyes. Death will exist no longer; grief, crying, and pain will exist no longer; because the previous things have passed away.

Revelation 21:4
Holman Christian Standard Bible

ABOUT THE AUTHOR

Hisashi Nikaidoh, MD, Medical Director of Children's Hospital at Saint Francis in Tulsa, OK, earned his medical degree from The University of Tokyo in 1959 and trained at Mount Sinai Hospital, New York City; Children's Memorial Hospital, Chicago; and Case Western Reserve University Hospital, Cleveland. He served in Dallas as Professor of Cardiothoracic Surgery at the University of Texas Southwestern Medical Center and Chief of Pediatric Cardiothoracic Surgery at Children's Medical Center. Dr. Nikaidoh is internationally known for the innovative surgical procedure that carries his name and his life-long dedication to the care of children, for which he received the Children's Miracle Achievement Award in 2011. In addition, Dr. Nikaidoh has been a long-time teacher of the Gospel and served on multiple missions, domestic and abroad.

For more information about

HISASHI NIKAIDOH, MD
&
HEALING HEARTS
please visit:

www.TheHealingHeartsBook.com
author@TheHealingHeartsBook.com
www.facebook.com/TheHealingHeartsBook
www.twitter.com/HealingHeartsBk

For more information about
AMBASSADOR INTERNATIONAL
please visit:

www.ambassador-international.com
@AmbassadorIntl
www.facebook.com/AmbassadorIntl